BUSINESS AND FINANCE

for working in organisations

Dave Needham and Rob Dransfield

HEINEMANN EDUCATIONAL

Tutor's Pack

CONVERSION TABLE

This Tutor Pack has been written to go with the first edition of Business and Finance, as it has proven so successful we have revised and expanded this current edition. You will find below, for your convenience, a table of page equivalents for conversion.

Also note that chapter 10 in the first edition becomes chapter 11 in the revised edition, for chapter 11 now read chapter 12 and so on ... chapter 18 is now chapter 19 etc.

1st Ed.	Rev. Ed.	1st Ed.	Rev. Ed.	1st Ed.	Rev. Ed.	1st Ed.	Rev. Ed.	1st Ed.	Rev. Ed.	1st Ed.	Rev. Ed.
2	2	76	81	143	150	198	232	265	313	352	408
3	3	77	82	144	151	201	235	267	315	353	409
4	4	78	83	145	152	202	236	269	317	355	413
5	5	81	86	146	153	203	237	272	320	356	414
12	12	82	87	147	154	204	238	274	322	357	415
13	13	84	89	148	155	205	239	275	323	359	417
18	18	86	91	149	156	206	240	276	324	360	418
19	19	87	92	150	157	208	242	277	325	365	423
23	23	88	93	151	158	209	243	278	326	367	425
26	26	89	95	152	159	212	246	280	331	368	426
27	27	90	96	153	161	213	247	283	334	369	427
28	28	91	97	154	162	214	248	284	335	370	428
29	29	92	98	155	163	215	249	286	337	371	429
30	30	93	99	156	164	216	250	287	338	372	430
32	34	94	100	158	166	217	251	288	339	377	437
33	35	97	103	159	167	218	252	289	340	379	439
34	36	98	104	160	168	219	253	292	343	383	443
35	37	99	105	161	169	220	254	295	346	384	444
37	39	100	106	162	170	222	256	299	353	385	445
39	41	102	108	163	171	223	257	300	354	386	446
40	42	104	110	164	172	224	258	301	355		
41	43	109	113	165	173	225	259	302	356		
42	44	111	116	168	176	226	260	303	357		
43	45	112	117	169	177	227	261	306	360		
44	46	113	118	171	180	229	263	308	362		
45	47	114	119	172	181	231	274	312	366		
46	48	115	120	173	182	232	275	313	367		
47	49	116	121	174	183	233	276	314	368		
48	50	117	122	175	184	234	277	318	372		
49	51	118	123	176	185	236	279	320	374		
50	52	122	127	178	187	237	280	324	378		
52	55	123	128	179	188	238	281	325	379		
53	56	124	129	181	190	239	282	327	383		
54	57	125	130	183	192	240	283	328	384		
55	58	126	131	184	193	241	284	329	385		
57	60	129	134	185	194	242	285	330	386		
58	61	130	135	186	195	243	286	332	388		
59	62	131	136	187	196	246	289	333	389		
60	63	132	137	188	222	250	293	334	390		
61	64	133	138	189	223	253	301	335	391		
62	65	134	141	190	224	254	302	336	392		
65	68	135	142	191	225	257	305	338	394		
66	69	136	143	192	226	258	306	339	395		
67	70	137	144	193	227	259	307	340	396		
70	75	138	145	194	228	260	308	341	397		
71	76	140	147	195	229	261	309	344	400		
74	79	141	148	196	230	262	310	346	402		
75	80	142	149	197	221	263	311	348	404		

CONTENTS

SECTION 1

1	Introduction	4
2	Planning, Implementation and Evaluation	5
3	Working in Organisations	8
4	Integrating Skills with Knowledge and Understanding	8
5	Developing Your Own Case Studies	10
6	Working in Groups	12
7	Using Simulation as a Teaching Tool	14
8	Work Experience	16
9	Using Local Industry as a Resource	18
10	Integrating Information Technology into the Course	19
11	Using a Keywords Approach to Developing Business Terminology	21
12	Helping Students to Learn Through Sharing Information by Card Games	22
13	Using Overhead Transparencies (OHPs)	22

SECTION 2

- Parts A to F each contains an *introductory discussion* and *supporting notes*.
- Each chapter is provided with five or six *full-size OHPs* with explanatory notes.
- Part D has additional *student activities*.

Part A – The Working World

Chapter 1	The Organisation	24
Chapter 2	Working for an Organisation	31
Chapter 3	The Needs of the Employee	39

Part B – The Client

Chapter 4	Assessing Customer Needs	46
Chapter 5	The Market-place	53
Chapter 6	Marketing Products and Services	60

Part C – The Administration

Chapter 7	Communication	67
Chapter 8	Using Information Technology in Organisations	74
Chapter 9	People in their Working Environment	81

Part D – Performance

Chapter 10	Financial Resources	88
Chapter 11	Understanding Financial Statements	95
Chapter 12	Using Information for Forecasting	102
● STUDENT ACTIVITIES		111

Part E – The Wider Business Environment

Chapter 13	External Influences on the Organisation	126
Chapter 14	The Environment of Change	133
Chapter 15	Organisational Responsibilities	141

Part F – Managing the Organisation

Chapter 16	Producing Goods and/or Services	149
Chapter 17	Making the Most of People	156
Chapter 18	Reviewing Performance	164

Glossary 173

SECTION 1

1 Introduction

Business and Finance has been written specifically to support tutors and learners following the BTEC National course of the same name. Programmes leading to BTEC qualifications aim to provide a broad educational foundation which will equip students for a range of careers in a rapidly changing world. The programmes are designed to be intellectually challenging and to assist students to cope with all aspects of the working environment.

Students can be supported in developing this 'broad educational foundation' by actively engaging in a practical enquiry process involving tasks, assignments, study of cases, simulations, role play, practical experience and other appropriate methods of active discovery learning.

The BTEC National Certificate and Diploma courses are designed to provide students with knowledge, understanding and skills essential to employment in business in the private and public sectors, plus the opportunity to specialise in particular areas of choice. They promote personal effectiveness through the practical application of studies, enhancing career prospects and providing a sound basis for progression to further studies in higher and professional education.

The aims of our publication are therefore designed to replicate those of the BTEC approach, namely to:

- develop vocational skills, knowledge and understanding which enable learners to be competent and immediately effective in employment in organisations in the public and private sectors
- provide a foundation for a range of careers and the ability to transfer skills to different working environments
- provide a basis for and encourage progression to further studies in higher education and the professions
- assist learners to be flexible in response to the changing demands of business and society
- enhance learners' motivation and provide the opportunity for the development of personal qualities relevant to supervisory and managerial work
- promote in learners a positive and dynamic approach towards working in business and the public sector

(*BTEC National in Business and Finance: Guidelines and Core Modules*, April 1992)

The BTEC National qualification is intended for students who are currently employed or anticipating employment in a range of occupations in business and financial administration in industry, commerce and the public services. The occupations typically include:

- responsibility for own work, including negotiating and agreeing targets
- contact with customers internal and external to the organisation
- a broad range of complex tasks involving variables
- some control and supervision over the work of others
- responsibility for routine tasks with limited supervision, and involvement in non-routine tasks with greater levels of supervision

(*Ibid*, page 4)

The BTEC approach clearly lends itself to the development of a course which interweaves PROCESS, SKILLS and CONTENT. Students preparing for employment in business and financial administration need to explore ideas related to a number of important areas of business life: they need to explore theories relating to the running of organisations, and to be aware of legal frameworks, wider environmental issues and many other areas.

This range of background knowledge and investigation cannot be gained solely by on-the-job work experience. Students also need to have opportunities to work together to explore a range of contexts and cases. In particular they need to discover inter-relationships between politics, economics, society, technology, the law and the natural environment. We want all our students to be *critical thinkers*. By developing critical insights they can become more effective members of organisations. They need to be active decision makers: BTEC National students should be able to make contributions to discussions and to become involved in decision making processes using the basis of concrete underpinning knowledge. They need to be able to take on board ethical and environmental issues as well as financial and marketing ones: we are looking for broad thinkers.

The BTEC National Core is made up of eight modules:

Module 1 Business Structures and Goals
Module 2 Business Environment
Module 3 Marketing Process
Module 4 Physical Resources
Module 5 Financial Resources
Module 6 Human Resources
Module 7 Administrative Systems
Module 8 Innovation and Change

We have tackled these modules in an integrated fashion. The grid below shows where each of these modules is covered in the text.

	1	2	3	4	5	6	7	8	9	10	11	12	13	14	15	16	17	18
Core Module 1																		
1.1	●	●																
1.2	●									●	●					●	●	●
1.3	●	●					●		●	●	●	●						●
1.4	●	●		●	●	●	●	●	●	●	●	●	●	●			●	●
Core Module 2																		
2.1	●				●	●			●	●			●		●		●	
2.2	●												●		●		●	
2.3		●				●			●				●					
2.4	●														●			
2.5		●				●							●	●				
Core Module 3																		
3.1				●	●													
3.2				●		●							●			●		
3.3				●	●	●		●					●	●		●		●
3.4				●	●	●							●	●		●		
3.5					●	●												
Core Module 4																		
4.1										●						●		
4.2										●						●		
4.3										●						●		
Core Module 5																		
5.1										●								
5.2										●		●						
5.3										●	●	●						
5.4										●	●	●						
Core Module 6																		
6.1	●		●				●						●			●	●	
6.2		●	●											●		●	●	●
6.3	●	●	●		●	●	●	●	●				●	●		●	●	●
Core Module 7																		
7.1	●	●	●			●		●							●			
7.2	●	●				●		●							●			
7.3	●	●		●		●			●	●			●	●		●	●	
7.4			●			●								●				
Core Module 8																		
8.1	●			●	●									●	●	●		●
8.2		●											●	●	●	●		●
8.3						●							●	●	●	●		●
8.4																		
Themes from Book	The Working World			The Client			The Administration			Performance			The Wider Bus. Environment			Managing the Organisation		

Good practice in BTEC National delivery involves providing activities which combine a number of objectives and underpinning knowledge and skills through the performance of real or simulated work-based TASKS and work-related ASSIGNMENTS. This is a major thrust of the text.

As well as providing a host of Case Studies and Tasks, we provide opportunities for students to consider their own skills and personal development. Students are encouraged to make presentations, to carry out research, to communicate effectively, to work in teams, to manage their own time, and to develop a range of other work-related competencies (such as IT capabilities).

2 Planning, Implementation and Evaluation

One of the key areas of development for students that we stress in *Business and Finance* is Planning, Implementation and Evaluation. This is equally important for long-term planning and for short-term action planning.

The PIE MODEL is particularly important for tutors engaged in the development and delivery of BTEC courses. Planning, teaching and assessment are inextricably linked: assessment informs a department's planning process, and thus feeds back into future teaching – as shown in the illustration.

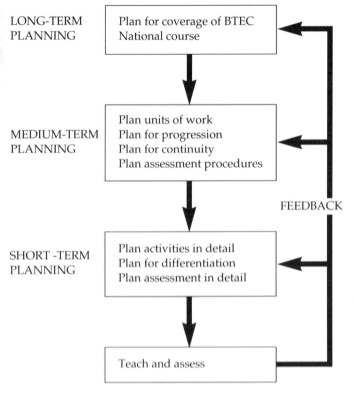

Long-term planning

Long-term planning involves a department or course committee in discussion about faculty/school or college curriculum policies. On the basis of this discussion staff are able to identify departmental aims and policies – for example, ways of linking with other courses.

Effective delivery of a subject or course begins with the department's plans to cover the appropriate course content detailed in a scheme of work. It should be broad and balanced, allowing for a range and variety of experiences. It should take into account continuity and progression by looking at the sequence of learning experiences, how learning can be reinforced and built upon.

Medium-term planning

A business studies department, faculty or school should then be able to identify units of work, topics or themes upon which to base its teaching and learning programmes. This can only be done by you, because you will need to make use of your local business environment. At this point a range of suitably differentiated activities can be devised and the assessment opportunities identified, so that all students are given the opportunity to meet the course objectives.

Short-term planning

Short-term planning is the responsibility of the individual tutor. This will be set in the context of many important factors:

- *The tutor's view of what is important about the subject.* Every tutor will have a perspective of what should be taught, and how it can best be taught, and how learners can best be supported.
- *The needs of the learner.* Students come into a classroom with varying requirements and needs. it is important to find out what these are in order to provide the best support to each learner.
- *The requirements of the course specifications or syllabus.* These are expressed by BTEC in terms of principal objectives, range statements, and indicative content, as well as core skills and competency statements.
- *The tutor's immediate aims.* The tutor will have the clearest picture of where students have come from and the steps required to take them forward. Building up a student profile which involves the ACCREDITATION OF PRIOR LEARNING helps to give a detailed picture. Clearly this takes time, but it helps to build up a better understanding of pathways that can be followed. As the course facilitator, the tutor will be providing learning opportunities, and monitoring students' progress in order to take learners forward. The process of gauging the development of students is very important. The tutor's aims will be based on this knowledge of prior learning, student characteristics, curricular aims and assessment tasks.
- *Common skills.* Lesson planning will also need to take these into account.

Organising an assignment

An important vehicle for learning is assignment-based work. If you set out an ACTION PLAN to prepare for an assignment, you can then more clearly reflect on the PIE processes involved.

For example the action plan could take the following form. Suppose that the planned assignment looks at health and safety at work and involves research based on actual work experience as well as library and other research.

- AREA FOR DEVELOPMENT. Set out the aims and objectives of the assignment – the skills and content that you want to develop. This will give you a clear idea of what students are expected to do, and why (e.g. to explore health and safety obligations and requirements in a chosen workplace; to build up knowledge of the rights and obligations of employers and employees; to develop awareness and ability to carry out safe working practices). In the example developed below we assume that the course team designs the assignment structure in conjunction with colleagues in various workplaces. (Of course, a similar assignment could be negotiated with students so that the learners take a greater responsibility for assignment design.)
- THE TEAM. Name the persons responsible for developing the assignment (the tutor/course team).
- TASK GROUP. Who will support you in developing the learning activity? This may be a group of tutors and colleagues in the workplace (e.g. a Health and Safety Officer, a Supervisor etc.).
- STATEMENT. This should explain what the task group is set to achieve. The statement should be a short description of the purpose and organisation of the assignment.
- ROLES. Who should do what in the task group? What are the responsibilities of the tutor/course team/industrial colleagues/groups of students/individual students?
- ANALYSIS OF NEEDS. This can be a short SWOT analysis setting out factors supporting the likely success of the assignment development, and barriers to be overcome. It will highlight any difficulties and ways of overcoming them.
- ACTION STEPS. Tutors, organisational members, etc. can then identify the main steps required to complete successfully the

structuring, organisation, delivery and evaluation of the assignment. Steps should be set out in order of importance.
- EVALUATION. Identify at the outset the criteria that will be used to assess the success of your action steps, because you will need to know how to measure your success. Clearly the task group can support each other in this venture.

Implementation

Useful guidance as to implementation of the Business and Finance course is provided by BTEC: 'There is a temptation when faced with outcome specifications to try to deliver each outcome separately. However, such a programme when applied to the core modules is likely to appear disjointed to the majority of learners who require the whole core, and may fail to make essential relationships between core areas.' In our text, therefore, we combine an integrated approach to the core with the ability to pick out whatever sub-components an individual learner might require.

A method recommended by BTEC pilot centres – and one suited to Business and Finance – is that of delivering the core by a series of ACTIVITY BLOCKS programmed over varying periods of time according to their individual scope and coverage. The outcomes and the range of underpinning knowledge and skills covered in each block are mapped by the course team and provide a bank of learning opportunities and associated assessment opportunities.

Features of a block delivery system

Extracts from *BTEC National in Business and Finance: Guidelines and Core Modules*, April 1992:

A Each block can best be designed around a broad business theme; e.g. the formation of a business, expansion and diversification, managing change, relocation of a business, organising a conference. Blocks may vary in length from perhaps 2 – 3 weeks (e.g. induction) to perhaps 7 – 8 weeks (e.g. expansion into Europe). Mapping of the learning opportunities built into each block will ensure coverage of the specified core outcomes, across the full range required. Much of the period spent on a block can normally be considered as formative, with summative assessment coming towards the end. It is wise to arrange for outcomes to be repeated (in different contexts) in different blocks so that they can be revisited by students to confirm and reinforce achievement.

B Each block should contain a number of related activities, assignments and simulations which provide the basis for the achievement and assessment of outcomes. Care should be taken to ensure the systematic development of COMMON SKILLS. The activities should:
   a be based on a real organisation or a realistic simulated one
   b provide learners with real or realistic roles
   c use a balance of different assessment methods appropriate to the activities undertaken
   d be mapped by type and coverage against the qualification profile of outcomes, performance criteria and range.

C Overall, the design of the block delivery programme should be such that:
   a the required module outcomes are carefully mapped across the activities, giving learning and assessment opportunities which overall allow complete coverage of performance criteria across the required range for each outcome
   b the assessment evidence is securely captured and recorded when it occurs
   c after induction and Accreditation of Prior Learning, students can take ownership of their own developing profile, being pro-active in sharing the planning of their way forward and the gathering of evidence to support the claim of achievement
   d there is a periodic individual review leading to individual action plans through which students can identify their personal targets for the next phase and their means of achievement.

(*BTEC National in Business and Finance: Guidelines and Core Modules*, April 92)

There are many ways of implementing and delivering the core areas of a Business and Finance course. Course teams will choose the method which is best for the team, for external partners and for the needs of the learners. Some teams will want to develop courses which involve a lot of planning and organised activities, whereas other courses will be highly flexible and will be 'worked out' by ongoing negotiation between tutors and learners. There are many different models which are likely to be highly effective – what works will be what suits your course team and your students. However, all successful courses will need detailed planning structures, clearly defined roles, clarity about assessment procedures, and a careful blending of process, skills and content.

The BTEC guidelines which are referred to in this section provide several useful delivery models for full-time and part-time courses. All these models can be effective and would work well with our text. For example, you will be able to see clearly that the typical block of 6 – 8 weeks suggested here fits well with the text.

Example of a typical block (6 – 8 weeks)

Block 1 (Theme 1)				Block 2
1 Week	3 – 5 Weeks	1 Week	1 Week	1 Week
Intro APL Credit	Learning Programme Mini activities (formative)	Major activities (summative)	Feedback	Intro etc.

Each thematic block is broken down into four stages:

a Introduction to thematic block

   Learners are introduced to the anticipated outcomes of the block and the skills required to complete it successfully. A significant feature of this first stage of the first block is the accreditation of prior learning.

b The learning programme

   The learning programme comprises:
   - multidisciplinary knowledge inputs through a variety of methods, eg formal, workshop, case study
   - preparatory activities and assignments which reinforce learning and form the basis of the formative assessment

c Major activity

   The major activity provides summative assessment for the whole block. However, it also offers further learning opportunities and seeks to reinforce knowledge and skills already developed.

d Feedback

   An essential feature of the block approach is the individual feedback through tutorial and counselling which provides opportunities for reviewing individual achievement of outcomes and updating the personal profile. The tutorial also seeks to identify individual strengths and weaknesses and contribute to preparation for the next block. Pilot experience has shown that a blurring between blocks can occur: there is often no clear distinction between feedback from one block and introduction to the next.

- provide a mechanism by which a course can be integrated
- encourage courses to be student-centred active-learning experiences
- reinforce and support the assignment approach.

The development of themes from the summary of outcomes in the core specification should be viewed as central to the successful integration of both knowledge and understanding as well as vocationally specific and common skills. For instance, in the same way that schemes of work are drawn up to relate to each theme so that the range in each outcome can be achieved, considerable thought at the planning stage must also be applied to identify exactly how and where skills can be integrated into the course structure. The Tasks in *Business and Finance* draw on the full range of common skills.

Applying skills

The aim for any course is to create situations in which skills can be developed in an occupational area so that they can then be transferred to working life. The most common method of doing this has been the unit assignment which, when linked with other units, has become an integrated assignment. Though this strategy has undoubtedly been successful, there are many problems associated with it. For example:

- More often than not the assignment is written first and the skills identified afterwards.
- The concept of skills comes across as being a woolly area for staff and students alike.
- Whereas students clearly understand the knowledge and understanding being assessed, they often feel that skills have only peripheral importance.
- Identifying where to integrate common skills in an assignment can be a hit and miss affair.
- With a large number of students, recording procedures can become extremely complex.

There are no instant solutions to such problems. Sometimes trying to cater for skills creates a sea of paperwork and the necessity to harangue staff constantly to ensure that such skills are being properly catered for.

One suggestion is that, if skills are to continue to assume great importance within the BTEC process – and there is no evidence to the contrary – teams should make a conscious effort to assess their importance and, where necessary, develop a repositioning strategy. There are many ways to do this. Meeting more often to discuss skills is perhaps the most obvious but, given the nature of the common skills draft specification, is this enough? The skills seem to involve a lot more, particularly when it comes down to evidencing competences and identifying how well the activities of each student cater for each range statement.

Another idea is to allocate more time to skills. Skills should continue to be assessed through the PIA programme, but a SKILLS WORKSHOP of some description could monitor and assess how each student is coping with such activities. A workshop of this description should not be perceived as a time for students to catch up or to take a break from routine: it should be viewed as an activity-centred experience which receives input from all of the other core modules. The availability of technology, meeting facilities and other resources would probably be very helpful.

One effective way of assessing skills is to provide a number of major skill-based activities within the course. In Chapter 13 of *Business and Finance*, on page 264, we mention that a period of work experience could be used to find out information and investigate activities based upon an assignment. It could also be used to assess skills in the workplace. For example, the skills tutor could interview the student on the work placement and also ask employers to provide a confidential assessment to develop your conclusions further. In this tutors pack we also suggest an assignment based upon a visit in which students have to take responsibility for finding out information about activities in order to complete their assignment. This is again a useful opportunity to assess skills.

On page 173 of the book we mention another idea for assessing skills. At Darlington College of Technology we were conscious of the need to put students in a different environment so that they could actively practise skills in a real situation where they would have to take more responsibility for their actions. In order to do so we decided to take them away (in the middle of February) to Howtown Outdoor Education Centre by the side of Lake Ullswater. The purpose of the visit was to assess whether or not such a situation could be used to develop skills, and for us to find out whether this could be regularly integrated into the course. The Case Study in the book assesses how we interpreted the feedback from students and staff alike. From this visit we developed the following assignment which we could give to other groups attending the course.

PIA – COMMON SKILLS ASSESSMENT

'Using outdoor education to develop and assess business skills'

During your diploma course you are regularly assessed upon a range of business skills for which you receive grades (see skills statement). These skills play an essential role in developing your effectiveness in both adult and working life. As the business world is constantly changing (specially with the development of new products, services and technologies), all workers require a certain degree of competence to enable them to adapt and respond to such changes.

The purpose of this assignment is to provide a means of assessing these business skills by giving opportunities to tackle a range of problem-solving exercises using outdoor activities. Another feature of this assignment is to enable you to assess where your strengths and weaknesses lie so that you can do something about them.

TASK

You are to attend a 5-day (5-night) residential course at Howtown Outdoor Education Centre by the side of Lake Ullswater, Penrith in Cumbria, commencing Monday and returning Saturday. During this time you will be assessed on a range of business skills from the skills statement, by the Howtown centre staff.

a Fill in immediately *Questionnaire 1* making your answers as detailed as possible.
b At the end of your stay at the Howtown centre you will be asked to fill in *Questionnaire 2*, which is designed to make you think about the nature of the skills development during the course. This will be followed up by a support interview back at college and a personal report from the Howtown centre staff.

Developing Your Own Case Studies

Questionnaire 1
CONFIDENTIAL

1. Name ....
2. College Group ....
3. Age ....
4. a. How important are the skills mentioned in the 'Skills Statement' for business employers/employees?
   b. Give examples to illustrate how they might prove useful.
5. What strengths or weaknesses do you feel you have in each of the skills?
6. In what way(s) do you think problem-solving activities help to develop the skills mentioned?
7. a. Give details of any previous problem-solving activities you have experienced (e.g. school visits, Duke of Edinburgh Award Scheme, Scouts or Guides, sporting activities, academic success).
   b. In what ways do you feel you benefited from the experience you mentioned in part (a).
8. Describe the skills you required to succeed in the activities you described in question 7.

Questionnaire 2
CONFIDENTIAL

1. Name ....
2. College Group ....
3. Age ....
4. Name of Instructor ....
5. a. Which activities did you find easiest? Why?
   b. Which activities did you find most difficult? Why?
6. How effectively did your group work together during the week? Why?
7. List the activities from which you benefited most/least during the week.
8. In what ways did you feel you benefited/did not benefit from the course?
9. How would you improve the course at Howtown?

The importance of skills

We hope that this short extract has made you think a little bit more about the importance of skills and about how they could be viewed. Skills are an opportunity to develop a course further with more exciting practical activities which enable both you and your students to gain more from the experience.

5 Developing Your Own Case Studies

In *Business and Finance* we present many Case Studies, most of which are taken from real situations. Case Studies are particularly valuable as learning tools because they help students to get inside real problems and decision making situations. They face real data, and need to make sense of it and take it apart. Cases need to be chosen for their interest. They need to relate to the interests of young people, to be easy to 'visualise', and to provide opportunities for students to practise their developing business understanding and skills. Abstract cases about theoretical 'widgets' are unlikely to fire anyone's imagination, and statistics about some fictitious electronics factory making highly esoteric products will send most of us to sleep. When people in working organisations tackle problems they normally get the opportunity to 'see' the problem for themselves. Cases need to bring home this external reality of a problem.

We suggest that in addition to using the Case Studies in the text, you also develop some of your own materials.

Example 1 – Health and Safety

Case Studies are most effective when students get the opportunity to actually 'visit' the case. For example, a group of students studying food safety were given some background materials about Fenland Foods, a food processing company.

FOOD SAFETY

The recipe dishes sold at the food counters of shops like Marks & Spencer are made in modern food factories.

Fenland Foods makes cook-chill recipe dishes. The factory is situated on the edge of Grantham.

At least 35 different products are made in the factory every day. They are made exclusively for Marks & Spencer.

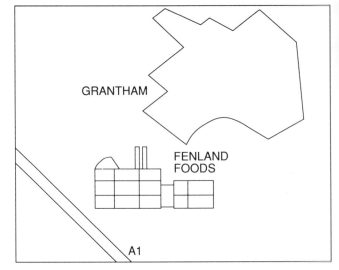

The recipe dishes must meet the very high standards that Marks & Spencer (and customers) set. Examples of recipe dishes include:

Braised Steak   Chili Con Carne
Cannelloni   Pork Roast, etc.

The giant kitchen of Fenland Foods goes on chopping, mixing, steaming, boiling and baking 24 hours a day six days a week. It is only on Saturday that the plant stops producing. Maintenance is carried out on Saturday.

Hygiene and cleanliness is of great importance in the food industry. All staff must be trained in safe working practices before they can start. Though it is hot in the cookhouse, other work areas are cool and the fridges icy cold. Hygiene and safety standards are rigidly enforced and cleaning is continuous.

From the moment a Fenland employee enters the factory, he or she must follow food safety rules. Here are some examples of the many rules that all employees must know.

PERSONAL WORKING PRACTICES

1. Do not smoke on the site.
2. Wash your hands properly
   - before starting work
   - after every break
   - after wiping your nose
   - after sneezing
   - after using hoses
   - after cleaning down
   - after touching the floor or anything that has been on the floor
   - before touching products
   - after using the lavatory.

3 All cuts, grazes and burns must be covered with the correct blue detectable waterproof dressings.
4 Do not take cigarettes, matches, purses, wallets and sweets into the workplace.
5 Do not take pins, needles or staples into the workplace.
6 Do not put your hands in your pockets.
7 Do not eat in the work place unless it is your job to do so.
8 Use a disposable tissue to wipe your nose. Place in waste bin and wash your hands.
9 Do not put your fingers in your nose, mouth or ears while working.

The flow chart shows the stages involved in changing for work.

Outdoor changing room

All employees remove coats/hats, lock away large bags, personal possessions and umbrellas.

↓

Go to

↓

Indoor changing room

1 Remove wellingtons, hat and hair net from personal locker.

↓

2 Put shoes in locker. Lock valuables (i.e. jewellery, wallets, purses) in locker.

↓

3 Put hair net and hat on.

↓

4 Put wellingtons on.

↓

5 Wash hands.

↓

6 Put coat on and fasten properly.

↓

7 Walk down stairs into production area. Walk through footbath.

↓

8 Wash hands and rub on debac solution (an ointment that kills germs).

↓

9 Enter production area.

After studying the background materials about safety at Fenland Foods, students can be asked to consider a number of questions:

- Why is food safety so important?
- Why are the working practices outlined so important?
- Who is responsible for safety in the workplace?
- What does the management of a food processing company need to do to ensure that food safety is fostered and developed?
- How can safety be viewed using a systems model approach?(see Chapter 1 of *Business and Finance*).

Clearly the materials make interesting reading and all students will take a direct and personal interest in the details of food safety. Perhaps as a comparison students should be asked to compare the factory system with food safety in the home.

Having studied the case materials students will benefit enormously from visiting the factory and observing food safety in action. As part of their visit they would go through the changing procedures, and be alert to observe working practices. This sort of direct personal Case Study really enriches a BTEC National course.

Example 2 – Meeting a Business Problem

A member of the local business community can be invited to pose a real problem to your class. The problem then becomes the focus for an assignment. When students have tackled the problem and produced a written report they can invite the problem-setter to come into the class to hear and see a presentation on how the problem has been tackled.

The Case Study below was constructed around a young entrepreneur in Aberdeen who was setting up his own pizza business.

How do I get planning permission for my new business?

The fast food business is very successful and can be very profitable. The demand for take-away pizzas, hamburgers, fried chicken etc. spread like wildfire in England during the 1980s. The market in Scotland has tended to follow after a period of time. Take-away Chinese food, for example, took off south of the border in the 1970s before spreading north. In Scotland the market is somewhat different because the Scottish fish and chip shop caters for a wider variety of tastes than its English counterpart, offering a vast selection of pies, puddings, pasties, deep-fried pizzas as well as different kinds of fish and chips.

Donald Ross thought that there was a market for take-away pizzas in Aberdeen, and in January 1989 he opened up *Don's Dial-a-Pizza*. He chose the name 'Don's' because, as well as being his own name, it is the name of the river in Aberdeen and the local football team. It also has appropriate Italian associations (pizza is an Italian dish).

Donald had originally hoped to set up in business in 1987. He had done a lot of research into the market. He studied government statistics and those produced by the pizza trade itself. The figures showed the two main markets were young people, particularly students and housewives under the age of 25 living in rented accommodation.

Donald went through the necessary calculations and decided that he could make a tidy profit from a pizza business.

His next task was to find a good location. He went to the local library and looked up the housing register to find out which areas of the city had the greatest concentrations of privately rented houses. Armed with this information, he tramped the streets in those areas looking for suitable premises.

It was at this stage that things began to go wrong. He found suitable premises of the right size in the part of Aberdeen where large numbers of students lived.

However, he had not consulted the local residents or the local council. The environmental health laws state that take-away premises cannot have residential properties immediately next door to them.

Further, they should not become a nuisance to local people. A resident found out what Don was planning, and organised a petition to the local Council objecting to the proposed shop. The petition was signed by 30 people.

Don had learned the hard way how important it was to win the support of local residents and of council planning and environmental health officials. So he visited all the residents who had signed the petition to explain his case. Most came round to his point of view. He wrote a letter to the local council explaining that he was unemployed, and that his business provided a valuable local service.

However, his planning application was turned down because of:

- considerable local opposition – even though many of the original 30 protesters had changed their mind
- the problem of litter
- possible congestion caused by late-night traffic.

This setback could have finished off Donald's hopes, but he decided to modify his idea – i.e. changing to *Dial-a-Pizza* and concentrating on home delivery. The profit and loss calculations showed that this could be a paying concern, and provided he added 75p for delivery he could make a healthy profit. It was also much easier to get planning permission. He was eventually able to lease an industrial unit to carry out his manufacture not too far from residential areas. His pizzas went on to be very popular (so popular, in fact, that one day he was mugged, and the muggers left him with his money and ran off with two boxes of pizzas!).

Before giving the students an assignment task it is possible to review the materials by considering a number of questions:

1. How did Don spot a gap in the market? How did he make sure that this gap was worth filling?
2. Who was his target market? Why?
3. What factors influenced his choice of location?
4. What problems did he have in finding an appropriate location?
5. How did government regulations affect Don's chosen business?

The assignment

Donald found out that his original attempt to set up in business failed because of opposition by local people who complained to the council. He decided that he must win them all over to get their support for his plans.

He spoke to everyone who had signed the protest petition and wrote to the council, explaining that he was an Aberdonian, unemployed but enthusiastic and well-organised, with a fully-researched business idea. He had also adapted his plans. He abandoned the idea of an eat-on-the-premises pizzaria. Instead he proposed to run a delivered-to-the-home service only. This meant that there would be no litter and no congestion. The change in plan and the personal appeal to the local people and the council worked.

Imagine that you are Donald Ross:

1. What would you say to local residents to persuade them to accept your case? Prepare a set of arguments.
2. Compose a letter to the local planning authority asking permission to set up. Donald says that to do this you need to show that you are professional and business-like. In this letter, you should make it clear that you are an Aberdonian, that you have been unemployed for two years and that you have fully researched your market. The letter should be 'topped and tailed' as follows:

```
                                            Donald A Ross,
                                            43 Kirkbank,
The Planning Committee,                     Aberdeen,
Department of Planning and Building Control,   'postcode'
City of Aberdeen District Council.            (date)
St Nicholas House, Aberdeen

Dear Sirs,

        Re Planning Permission Reference No. 86/2199

              [Your letter goes here]

Yours faithfully,
Donald A. Ross
```

Conclusion

There can be no doubt that development of your own locally based Case Studies will capture the imagination of your students.

The starting point is to look at local products and workplaces that you think will appeal to your students. The Business Section of the local paper often brings to light interesting cases. Ring up a contact person at a local business – usually the personnel manager. Arrange to meet them, and ask if you can go round the premises. Show how enthusiastic you are about building links. Highlight areas of interest as you tour the business site. Establish some clear objectives for Case Study and partnership work. Then either write the Case Study yourself or in conjunction with your industrial partner. Try to couple the study with a student visit to the business being studied. Make sure that your students provide plenty of positive feedback about the link.

6 Working in Groups

Many activities and assignments on a Business and Finance course can be carried out by groups of students working together. An important part of the course therefore involves introducing students to teamwork skills, and helping them to be aware of the benefits of teamwork, and how they personally fit into a team.

The tutor may encourage groups of students to set up a team base at the start of a course. The team base would house work resources such as work stations, folders, texts, business dictionaries etc. The tutor would need to establish a working pattern with the group whereby they manage their own working relationships; e.g. who is responsible for particular research tasks, the sharing of research information, who responds to memos from the course tutor?

What is a team?

It is helpful for groups to arrive at a working definition of 'team' at an early stage in the course; e.g.:

'A team is a small group who have developed to the stage where they are able to perform effectively, each member adopting the role necessary to work with others, using complementary skills.'

At an early group meeting students may benefit from carrying out a SKILLS AUDIT (a record of the skills which each member of the group possesses). Another useful exercise is for students to think about other groups that they belong to, trying to draw out ways in which the groups are similar or different.

In looking at what makes a group, students will notice that for a group to exist it must identify itself as a group (e.g. the Mountaineering Club, the Gary Glitter Appreciation Society, a student sub-culture etc.) In addition there needs to be (examples relate to a student sub-culture):

- a set of written or unwritten rules, known to the group members (e.g. an accepted way of dressing)
- some form of sanction for breaking rules (e.g. being ignored by other group members)
- a common aim or purpose (even if just to have a good time mixing with each other at college)
- form of communication (e.g. a set way of greeting each other)
- ways for group members to identify themselves as belonging to the group (e.g. status symbols, patterns of speech, hairstyles etc.)
- ways by which individuals can achieve their own goals as a part of the group, for them to continue membership (e.g. to enjoy friendship while gaining a useful qualification).

Having established what a group is, students can go on to focus on what a 'team' is. They will, it is hoped, see a team as a small, well developed group. Students can be asked to brainstorm ideas as to what makes a good team/teamwork; e.g.:

- closeness
- loyalty to the group
- good knowledge of each other (including strengths and weaknesses)
- accepted ways of behaving
- good time management
- high levels of communication
- freedom to express opinions and feelings
- complementary skills and roles
- group language and jargon

If students are going to work well together as a group they will need to develop many (if not all) of these teamwork skills. Teamwork and cooperation with others towards a common goal will help students develop insights into processes such as conflict, cooperation and consensus. At the same time participants may learn about leadership skills and some of the practices associated with authority.

A group activity

Many different activities can be carried out at the beginning of a course to encourage groups of students to share ideas and working practices. Here is an example:

Your Business Studies tutor has asked students to work in a group of three on an assignment that will take six weeks. The assignment is based on finding out why new companies have located on an industrial estate on the edge of your town. For the assignment individual students will need to interview managers at three companies, and share this data with the rest of the group. The group will then have to produce a group presentation in which they will all take part. The assignment must be produced to clear deadlines and involves hard work and group cooperation.

Which three of the following four group members do you think would make the best team? Working in groups of three or four students, read through the materials and then discuss each of the potential team members before making a decision:

Student A: Karen Greaves is hard-working and conscientious. She has had experience of working in an office for a small company. She is a Guide Leader and has won several leadership badges. At times she can be a bit overpowering and may dominate other members of the group.

Student B: Winston Roberts is a quiet student who produces good-quality work to tight deadlines. He also has the knack of coming up with bright and imaginative ideas. In his spare time he works as a taxi driver.

Student C: Saroj Panja is known to be a bit of a joker. At times he has a 'relaxed' attitude to work. His great ability is to pull other members of a team together. He can surprise people with his effort when 'the chips are down'

Student D: Mary Reynolds is an extremely hard working and serious student. She is a good sharer of ideas and will help others out. When not working on college tasks she tends to keep to herself.

Having carried out the activity described above, students can then discuss their responses. Did different groups come up with the same or different solutions to the problem? The tutor should then discuss how the groups worked together. What role did participants play in the discussions? Did some students tend to dominate discussions? What about the body language? etc.

How well a team works together depends in some measure on the mixture of personalities and abilities of group members. If everyone wants to lead or everyone wants to follow it is unlikely that the group will interact very well together.

Robert Belbin identified eight roles which may be crucial to teamwork. Of course, individuals will take on more than one of these roles at different times during a course.

The **chairperson** presides over the group, and coordinates team efforts. The **shaper** is a would-be chair of the group. He or she drives the team on to successfully complete the task.

The **plant** may be a rather shy person, but successful at creating ideas and new proposals.

The **monitor evaluator** is able to analyse a situation, to look at what is going on and to suggest ways forward. This person checks the quality of progress and makes pertinent comments.

The **resource investigator** is usually an extrovert who mixes well with other group members. He or she can bring new contacts and ideas to the team, which will need to be worked on by more methodical members of the group.

The **company worker** is a very hard worker who can turn ideas into manageable tasks. He or she tends to be good at administration rather than a leader.

The **team worker** is very good at supporting the team, by helping to encourage others and to support and harmonise the working of the team.

The **finisher** makes sure that tasks are completed, and deadlines are met. He or she does not allow unfinished business to be left waiting.

Clearly a blend of all these characteristics is important in teamwork.

The components of group working

Whenever groups of students work together, there will be three strands involved in moving from the start of the decision-making process to the finish. These strands are illustrated below:

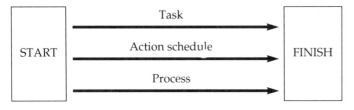

Task

The task is the content of the work – it is the conversion of information and opinions from members into decisions, recommendations, reports, or other outcomes. In general terms this covers what has to be done and why. Most groups give a lot of attention to the task.

Action schedule

The action schedule is concerned with how a group will be organised to do a given task. The schedule will cover such questions as who will fill the necessary roles and how progress will be checked and monitored. It will also deal with the procedures of decision making. In general, the action schedule will cover the 'where' and 'how' of decision making. Most groups will give some attention to their action schedule.

Process

The process is the interaction which takes place between members of a group. It is about how people work together. It involves interpersonal skills such as listening to others and helping others to join in a discussion. It involves expressions of feelings and the giving and receiving of feedback. In general it covers who does what and when. Many groups pay little attention to process.

The above three threads of group working are all important in group decision making. It is obvious that a group which concentrates on its action schedule and its process entirely may have a wonderful time but it may not achieve the tasks. In contrast, concentration purely on the task is likely to lead to arguments about how things should be organised, and inattention to group members' thoughts and feelings will lead to mishandled resources and misunderstandings.

Because teamwork is an important core skill, it is important to help learners to become aware of the three elements outlined above. This is particularly true of process, which is often neglected. Students can be encouraged to consider process by carrying out a number of group tasks in class at the beginning of the course. We have a number of suggestions:

PROCESS OBSERVERS. When small group tasks are carried out, some students can act as advisory process observers. These students can comment on such things as:

- Who initiated activities?
- Who supported others in the group by assisting them when appropriate?
- Who harmonised the group by seeking consensus and common purposes?
- Who listened to others and respected their contributions?
- Who collected and organised information for the group?
- Who facilitated progress by involving others?
- Who in the group was reliable? etc.

The information provided by the process observers can be used to reflect on group dynamics and group interaction.

PERSONAL PROFILES OF PROCESS SKILLS. Students can work on a profile of their own teamwork skills. At the beginning of the course they can be given sheets which help them to reflect on these skills. (Perhaps they could work in groups to construct the sheets.) The sheets would enable a student to say 'I am good at/quite good at/poor at:

- starting a discussion
- helping others to join in
- building bridges between team members
- knowing when to shut up; etc.'

Students should be asked to consider their development against this profile during the course. In this way they should become more aware of teamwork skills, and will become better group members during the course.

Conclusion

There can be no doubt that if students develop teamwork skills as part of their BTEC Business and Finance course they will become more competent in collaborating with people to achieve organisational goals, in such areas as:

- motivating others and helping them to operate as effective team members in achieving task objectives
- performing a variety of roles within a team
- appreciating that individuals and groups have differing perceptions of goals, and that there may be conflict between them
- carrying out their role and work with others in working to achieve organisational goals; and so on.

7 Using Simulation as a Teaching Tool

What is a business simulation?

A business simulation is a defined model of a situation in which realistic ROLE PLAY helps participants to understand the behaviour of a system over which they can develop strategies and evaluate performance.

It is not always possible to use the 'real thing' in a chosen teaching situation. For example, in preparing students for work experience we may want to practise a simulated job interview before students are faced with the real thing. The tutor may act out the part of a potential employer with a student playing the part of a would-be employee. The activity could be carried out in front of a group of students. The tutor would introduce the role play and ask students to look at particular points – e.g. body language, communication skills, questions asked and answered, social relations involved, etc. The tutor would then ask students for feedback, and would review the activity with the group.

Clearly, the activity described above is a very powerful learning tool because it can be:

- introduced with clear learning objectives being stated
- stopped at any point so that processes can be scrutinised
- used as a vehicle for preparation and confidence building
- controlled by both learners and tutor – the learner is free to ask questions and to make comments.

Furthermore, outcomes can be evaluated in the light of the stated objectives. It is also possible to make a video recording of such a simulation. Students can observe the way in which they acted, and explore ways of improving performance. We have found this to be a very useful vehicle for the development of the learner. The performance of interviewees has improved greatly as a result of the increased self-awareness that comes from critically examining a video recording.

A similar activity which we have used is to ask students to 'interview' a selected group of 'actors' (students from another course) for a 'mock' job. This involved the preparation of job descriptions, letters of application, CVs, job specifications, and interview criteria. The students involved in this activity were very serious about their work. They were able to develop a clearer picture of the processes involved in preparation for, and implementation of, the interview situation.

The examples outlined above help to support the case for the use of simulation and role play in the classroom. The lessons learnt and the process of learning can be as vivid as any experience of real working situations.

Simulation is most effective:

- when it is carefully planned, executed and debriefed
- involves all students in a participatory way – clearly students who observe and provide feedback are just as much participants as those involved in an acting role
- when it feels real – students feel that they are replicating a real situation rather than just playing a game.

Planning an activity

As the manager of the learning environment the tutor needs to know in detail how the simulation is going to be developed. Introducing a business game or simulation for the first time can be daunting, particularly if it is complex. *Wherever possible, it is advisable to test the materials beforehand or run through them on your own.* When you have done this you will have a clearer idea as to what will go on and when. Make sure that:

- the activity fits the objectives of the course
- you are aware of the likely outcomes and how these relate to your initial objectives (although you will always have a few surprises)
- you have identified the parts of the simulation which may need to be reinforced or for which help may be required
- you have planned a programme detailing when tutor inputs will be required (you may need to stop the simulation at particular stages and discuss what is going on and what has been learnt)
- there are enough copies of instructions, playing materials and other resources
- you have a good idea of the timing of the various sections of the simulation
- the simulation is at an appropriate level for the students you are working with.

Running the activity

The business game or simulation should have three main parts: the BRIEFING, the ACTIVITY, and the DEBRIEFING.

The *briefing* is the initial explanation by the tutor of the purpose, principles and rules of the simulation. Sometimes activities are designed to encourage regular briefings to assess progress, comment on performance and/or introduce information to change the direction of the activities. Documents read during the briefing may need to be consulted by students as an on-going part of activities. Instructions given to students should be clear. You will need to repeat key points, and to clarify objectives and time constraints (perhaps by writing them clearly on the whiteboard). You should allow students to clarify objectives by asking questions. *It is essential that the briefing is clear and that it is understood.* Without such an understanding the purpose and the actual running of the activity may lose much of its value.

During the *activity* the tutor becomes the controller in charge of the mechanics of the game or simulation. In this role the teacher needs to exert tight control over areas such as time constraints, the release of information, the interaction between groups, and the participation of all individuals. The beauty of such an activity is that, though the exercise is being carried out by young people who may have little experience of business activities, their thinking and their contributions to the decision-making processes are genuine and mirror reality. At times the tutor may need to advise groups on the implications of their decisions – although failure can be viewed in some circumstances as a valuable learning experience (we should be very wary of activities which give a sense of personal failure).

In the *debriefing* the controller reverts back to a teaching role. A thorough debriefing helps to bring out the lessons learnt and participants can more fully see connections with other parts of their business education. A useful method of gaining feedback is to get participants to give an oral presentation to the whole group – a participant from each group can present the group's work supported by a written report or the use of visuals such as flip-chart illustrations. Teachers can learn from the debriefing stage about the effectiveness of the simulation. This can help you to improve your organisation and presentation the next time you run the simulation.

Examples of business simulations

It is possible to argue that you can never fully simulate the real world. However, you could just as easily argue that decision making in the real world rarely follows the same pattern. No two problems are identical. What is more important is for students to learn and practise cross-transferable decision-making and problem-solving skills.

A frequently used type of simulation is that of a production exercise. There are many effective simulations which can be obtained from CRAC, Bateman Street, Cambridge CB2 1LZ. These cover a range of activities such as making underpants, paper hats, t-shirts, and many other products. You need to decide which simulation is most appropriate to the level of your students. Many production simulations can be used at varying levels of sophistication to incorporate such features as costings, break-even, marketing principles, and many others. A number of these activities are also available as computer-based simulations. The tutor needs to look at the learning objectives of such activities, the time involved, and the resourcing implications. Other popular simulations include:

Where to locate?
What to produce?
How to carry out market research?
Trade union negotiations
Government control over economic variables

Research-based simulations

The tutor can build simulations on the foundation of student research. For example, the tutor can introduce a trade union related activity by showing the class a local newspaper article on a current industrial dispute. The students can then be asked to research the issue and the perspectives of the two sides involved, by interview-based research, studying relevant newspapers and journals, and by researching the nature of industrial relations on a broader front. Students could explore the background and current history of trade unions. They could research types of industrial action, and the objectives of employer and employee-based organisations.

Given this background of research, students could be asked to form into groups to represent the employers' and the employees' sides in the case being studied. The students could then run a simulated meeting between the two sides armed with all the research information. During the simulated meeting all students can be asked to take on a second role – that of a newspaper reporter. The tutor can chair the meeting to make sure that all points are made clearly and slowly, as well as drawing out particularly relevant points. The meeting can attempt to resolve the issue in a logical way.

After the meeting the students could be asked to produce a newspaper report bringing out all the main issues. The newspaper report is particularly valuable in that it gives students an opportunity to draw out all they have learnt about trade unions, industrial relations and dispute procedures.

Such a simulation is a vital way of learning: it demands research skills, it demands thorough preparation, it demands effective communication. In return it provides enjoyment, real interest, understanding of local issues, the opportunity of learning by doing, and has the potential to empower students as important players in a democratic society.

Finding out what's on offer

Business and commercial work-related activities are particularly well suited to the use of games and simulations. Over recent years organisations in both the private and public sectors have made increasing use of such exercises for training purposes. Similarly in schools and colleges teachers have come to realise the educational merits.

Unfortunately, too often in the past many such resources have been produced either by firms for their own internal use, or by relatively small publishers producing low print runs, resulting in high prices. However, many large organisations today have education services which take an increasing interest in classroom activities and sponsor a wide variety of materials which include games and simulations for classroom use (e.g. UNISIM from Unilever Educational Liaison and the Enterprise Game from Shell Education Service). The larger publishers are also responding to the market by developing many resources for educational use, most of which are software-based. Two important sources of simulations are CRAC (see above) and Understanding Industry – which puts on short courses for schools and colleges introducing aspects of industrial life.

8 Work Experience

Planned work experience is an essential ingredient of any BTEC National course. During work experience, a student visits a place of work to watch and work alongside people who are earning their living. This provides an essential opportunity to develop and enhance CORE SKILLS. At the same time it provides a valuable context to carry out research and investigations for some of the assignment work on the course.

BTEC National courses involve a partnership between tutors, learners and employers. Work experience planning needs to involve these three groups so that aims and objectives can be established, action plans constructed, and learning outcomes monitored and assessed.

Some of the benefits of work experience for the learner are listed below:

1. The learner gets inside a workplace and has a feel of what it is like at work.
2. He or she develops cross-transferable general competencies which are relevant to any work situation (e.g. time management, teamwork, communication skills, decision making, and so on).
3. The learner can collect and experience real data for a BTEC National coursework assignment.
4. He or she finds out more about personal likes and dislikes. From doing work experience a learner might find out more about his or her suitability for different types of employment.
5. By going through the procedures of applying for a job and being interviewed, the learner gains good experience for the real thing.
6. Through work experience the learner should develop a clearer understanding of the inter-relationship between the theoretical and the practical aspects of the course.
7. The learner benefits from experiencing the independence and responsibility of working life.
8. The learner can ask questions of people at work who have practical experience.
9. He or she is able to develop new skills, and to use equipment and resources which are not available in a college environment.

Developing criteria for work experience

It is necessary to develop objectives and criteria so that the work experience can be planned and evaluated in a clear way. The development of criteria should be seen as an on-going exercise involving each party. Clearly, the work experience available in a particular area will depend on the characteristics of the local economy. At the present time the TECs are key players in this provision.

A representative from the local TEC will clearly be an important participant in a college-based partnership.

As with any other element of National courses, students need to be able to negotiate and discuss the expected outcomes of work experience with tutors involved. A placement supervisor from the college should visit the work placement prior to the work experience starting. Regular visits will then need to be made by the placement supervisor to discuss the learner's performance, both with the employers' representative and with the learner. Because of the sheer quantity of work experience involved with BTEC National, it may be necessary for the college to provide training to employers so that they can take over responsibility for a large part of the monitoring and assessment process. This has the added advantage of giving the learner the feel of being a real employee.

Preparation for work experience

An important purpose of work experience is to help students to prepare for the transition to full-time employment. One emphasis, therefore, will be on a careers element of work experience; i.e. developing skills, attitudes and understanding about different work situations to provide a general preparation for working life. Students will need to be aware of general vocational objectives. Most if not all working environments provide opportunities for reflection about the nature of working life. These opportunities need to be drawn out. Students will need to be fully briefed and prepared so that they can make the most of their work experience.

In addition, students can be asked to carry out specific investigations into their work organisations in order to meet other specific learning objectives of their course. In this case, it is essential that the specific aims and objectives are clearly spelt out; e.g.:

- examine the organisation's system of recruitment
- participate in an interview
- conduct an interview with a member of staff in order to investigate their job role
- produce an organisational chart
- find out about the Health and Safety responsibilities of employees.

Students will be placed in a wide variety of organisations, and it is essential that the objectives are clear. These objectives must be both achievable and flexible. For example, there would be little point in expecting a student to investigate the internal structure of British Telecom while work-shadowing a telephone linesman.

We present here a useful model for preparing work experience.

```
┌─────────────────────────────────────────────────────────┐
│ Invite a range of employer representatives to college to│
│ discuss aims and objectives of work experience.         │
│ Collectively negotiate general aims and develop into a  │
│ template                                                │
└─────────────────────────────────────────────────────────┘
                            ↓
┌─────────────────────────────────────────────────────────┐
│ Draw up a list of suitable employers and negotiate more │
│ specific objectives for work placements                 │
└─────────────────────────────────────────────────────────┘
                            ↓
┌─────────────────────────────────────────────────────────┐
│ Make a visit to the work place to fine-tune             │
│ requirements. You must make sure that your students are │
│ going into a safe working environment                   │
└─────────────────────────────────────────────────────────┘
                            ↓
┌─────────────────────────────────────────────────────────┐
│ Set up details by telephone or letter. Check on         │
│ insurance arrangements: insurance is essential.         │
└─────────────────────────────────────────────────────────┘
                            ↓
┌─────────────────────────────────────────────────────────┐
│ On-going preparation with students as a natural part of │
│ the course to (i) prepare them for work experience, and │
│ (ii) establish learning objectives and assessment       │
│ procedures                                              │
└─────────────────────────────────────────────────────────┘
                            ↓
┌─────────────────────────────────────────────────────────┐
│ Send letters and assessment forms to employers. If you  │
│ have not already done so, you will need to involve      │
│ employers in joint ownership of assessment of product   │
└─────────────────────────────────────────────────────────┘
                            ↓
┌─────────────────────────────────────────────────────────┐
│ Final student briefing                                  │
└─────────────────────────────────────────────────────────┘
                            ↓
┌─────────────────────────────────────────────────────────┐
│ Work experience placement                               │
└─────────────────────────────────────────────────────────┘
                            ↓
┌─────────────────────────────────────────────────────────┐
│ On-going assessment by tutors, employers and students   │
└─────────────────────────────────────────────────────────┘
                            ↓
┌─────────────────────────────────────────────────────────┐
│ Student outcomes                                        │
└─────────────────────────────────────────────────────────┘
                            ↓
┌─────────────────────────────────────────────────────────┐
│ Evaluation of outcomes by employers, students and tutors│
└─────────────────────────────────────────────────────────┘
```

Student preparation for work experience

Preparation for work experience is not a five-minute operation – it is a lengthy, practical and natural part of a course, involving preparation for interviews, discussion of work-based competencies, study of application techniques, and many other activities.

Students need to evaluate and when necessary to improve their production of a curriculum vitae and job application.

As part of work experience, students are normally expected to write a letter of application and then to attend an interview for a work experience placement. The employer will normally have the right to reject unsuitable applicants.

The student's letter of application should be addressed to the personnel manager, who will be looking for candidates:

a with the necessary experience (if experience is required)
b who express themselves clearly and in an organised way
c who show an enthusiastic interest in the work offered
d who have taken the trouble to find out what the work entails and something about the organisation.

Once personnel managers have selected who to interview they may send for references. It is therefore essential that students first seek permission from referees.

Students will need to be aware that there will be other applicants going for the work experience placement and that they will need to promote themselves as someone keen to get the vacancy.

In preparation for the work experience it may be helpful for all students to fill in a sheet giving clear details of the location, and details of people involved in the placement; e.g.:

Name of employing organisation..
Address of employer ....
Telephone number of employer and contact name ....
...
Person to whom responsible at work..
Date of reporting for work..............................Time................
Map to show place of work..

Performance at work

Students are expected to perform to certain standards at work in order to show general work proficiencies. These can be detailed in terms of outcomes, and students must be informed of the nature of the expected proficiencies at different levels of performance.

Indicators need to be established in order to record and assess performance. For example, a student may be involved in filing, invoicing, recording money transactions, and using the phone, in which case possible indicators are:

- recording transactions in a clear, correct and well organised fashion
- showing initiative in handling incoming phone messages; etc.

Students are also expected to meet established standards in their coursework related to work experience; e.g.:

- shows clarity of aims and objectives
- interviews several appropriate people at work
- records findings in an organised fashion
- draws out clear conclusions from study.

A student surveying a number of employees at work, for example, may go into the workplace with a set of pre-planned questions for investigation; e.g.:

Name of employee?
Job description?
Previous employment?
What do they enjoy about their work?
(student provides a list: e.g. good rate of pay, opportunities

for promotion, etc.)
What don't they like about their work?
What factors influence employee's attitude to work?

The student carrying out such an assignment would need to establish, in his or her coursework report, clear aims and objectives. These need to be established in negotiation with the tutor before the placement begins. A student who simply asks a list of prepared questions and writes down the answers with no analysis will clearly reap only limited benefits from the coursework. The assessment cycle should therefore be geared toward helping students to become aware of potential learning outcomes, and of ASSESSMENT CRITERIA.

The model for the student work experience should therefore fit the pattern shown here.

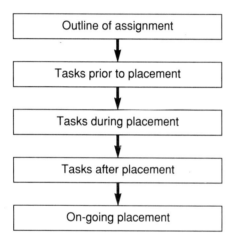

Monitoring and assessment

The tasks which students are asked to carry out before the placement act as monitoring devices, ensuring that they know something about the organisation before the initial contact. The requirement to draw up a checklist and questions ensures that they have done some preparation for the work ahead.

From these specific tasks students should be able to gather suitable material to use later. If the employer is already aware of these tasks then this will assist the student. Students are often required to keep a daily diary or log of their activities on work experience; this can be useful practice in logging information and can be submitted as evidence of the experience. It may be helpful for the college to produce a structured log book for students.

Students can also be asked to collect artefacts related to their work experience in order to assist them should they make a presentation to the rest of their group after their placement is completed.

Finally, it is essential that students are clear about how their work is to be assessed, what work they need to submit, when they need to submit the work and the criteria against which their work will be judged.

9 Using Local Industry as a Resource

An effective partnership with local organisations greatly enhances a BTEC National course. You may want to involve local industry in practical investigations in various ways.

Local Case Studies

Business and Finance is full of interesting Case Studies designed to capture the imagination of your students. However, your course will benefit from local studies; for example:

- Why did a certain firm set up in our town?
- What problems are faced by local high street businesses?
- How did company x obtain finance for expansion?
- How did the new bookshop discover that there was a market for its products?
- What were the ingredients of the business plan of this or that small business?

Some Case Studies can be written by lecturers, others by the students themselves. Activities, problems and tasks can be tackled by other groups of students. By working with small local organisations you can capture the imagination of students and operate at a level which is easy to penetrate. Clearly students will need to investigate business at local, regional, national and global levels.

However, the best way in to areas such as marketing, finance and human resource management is to take a good clear look at what is happening in your own backyard.

Surveying local industry

As part of the course, students need to look at regional economic patterns and trends. They can carry out this work by setting up a database holding information about employment patterns, types of local businesses, sizes of companies, major organisations etc. This database can then be used to support other learning activities on the course.

Setting tasks associated with local businesses

Many of the Tasks in *Business and Finance* invite students to carry out some research into, or to consider aspects of, local organisations. A number of integrated tasks can be used to provide valuable assignment work which will provide opportunities for you to make sure that learners can apply the underpinning knowledge and skills of the course.

For example, in Core Module 1: Working in a Group, students can carry out a survey of a large number of local businesses, storing information about type and purpose on a database. By interviewing key members of these organisations they can build up a picture of the goals and targets of a range of different organisations. At the same time the students could set up their own mini-company for a given period to provide goods or services. They could then contrast the goals and targets of their own organisation with ones that they have studied. They could also reflect on their own contributions as individuals and team members to the achievement of their stated business goals and targets.

As another example, in Key Module 3: Marketing Process, students could carry out a marketing project related to a product that is clearly increasing or declining in demand both locally and nationally (e.g. cinema attendance, video rental, purchase of satellite dishes). Ideally they would work as researchers for a local organisation to find out market trends. They would thus gather information to enable this organisation to evaluate the market. By carrying out research work, storing and sorting this information on a database, and looking at the impact of market forces, students will develop a clearer picture of the characteristics and operation of the market system. They can then develop a range of marketing responses to these changing external forces in order to maximise the marketing strength of the company. Students can produce a marketing plan which they can then present to their client organisation in a formal presentation.

Organising visits to local organisations

At its best, a visit to a local organisation can be a very powerful vehicle for learning. At its worst it will be an interesting distraction.

Visits should be carefully organised to maximise outcomes. The tutor needs to be clear as to:

- why the visit is taking place
- how the visit will be organised (administrative procedures)
- how the visit will be monitored and evaluated.

The tutor will therefore need to prepare the ground with the course team. Successful visits tend to be replicated (and improved on) year after year.

Students need to be provided with:

- background information about the trip and how it fits into the course
- housekeeping details (when to pay, what to wear, when to arrive, how to behave, what to bring)
- detailed objectives for the visit
- what they will have to do with the information (e.g. interview reports need to be written up on the evening of the visit)
- schedule for transforming the visit into finished coursework
- guidelines for follow-up.

Make sure that students are given a clear picture of how their report will be used. Will it form part of an assessed assignment? Perhaps the students could make a presentation to the company to show how they have benefited from the visit.

Developing work experience as part of the course

This is dealt with in more detail in Chapter 8. Work experience is of tremendous value, and in particular it supports the following outcomes:

1.3 Achieve business goals and targets
1.4 Contribute as an individual and team member to the achievement of business goals and targets
4.2 Audit physical resources in a work area
4.3 Make efficient and effective use of physical resources
5.3 Understand and interpret financial statements
5.4 Identify and assess the financial needs of an organisation and how they are met
6.1 Audit the human resources of an organisation
6.2 Investigate systems used to maintain and control human resources
6.3 Plan personal tasks and time efficiently
7.1 Identify roles and responsibilities of self and others in the organisational structure
7.2 Identify and use communication systems and administrative procedures and systems in organisations
7.3 Assess the applicability of, and where appropriate use, relevant technology in the operation of administrative procedures and systems
8.2 Assess the impact of change and innovation in a designated work area and working environment
8.3 Make and justify recommendations for change in an organisation.

Inviting local industrialists to give talks

It can be very helpful to use personal contacts of members of the course team to bring outside speakers into the BTEC National classroom. In addition, a number of organisations – such as the Banking Information Service – have their own trained speakers for educational purposes. You can also develop a more comprehensive programme by working with Understanding Industry.

Understanding Industry (UI) invites senior speakers from the world of business and industry to visit colleges and talk about a variety of carefully identified areas, such as human relations, marketing and management. Visits involve eight sessions and, though it is more common to organise sessions on a weekly basis, a particularly exciting format is to condense UI speakers for a course in a two-day conference. UI therefore aims to:

- provide 16 – 19 year old students staying on in education with a better understanding of industry and commerce
- operate within the college timetable
- work with tutors to develop UI as a curriculum resource
- involve business people in their local schools and colleges as part of a managed programme.

It is beneficial for students to be able to question specialists in a variety of fields. Most of the sessions involve active learning, simulations, games and role play.

10 Integrating Information Technology into the Course

Information processing is today a natural part of any Business Studies course. IT should be used as a tool to serve teaching, although students will need to keep a profile of IT skills which they will develop and enhance.

Because Business and Finance is taught in a student-centred manner, it becomes easier to integrate IT skill development. At the same time, opportunities to use IT takes pressure off the tutor – students develop their own working patterns at their individual or group work-stations.

As we have highlighted elsewhere, student-centred learning involves detailed preparation. The tutor becomes the manager or facilitator of the learning experience rather than its focal point. S/he gives an introduction to sessions and then provides students with assignments to act as a basis for their learning experience. You should exude an organised and purposeful air in order to encourage your students to work.

Many of the tasks in *Business and Finance* lend themselves to the use of IT applications, e.g.:

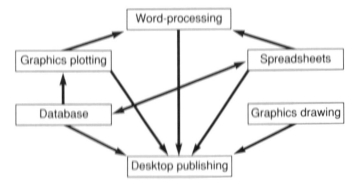

Integrating Information Technology into the Course

The tutor should offer advice on sources of information, provide help with the details of subject matter, and encourage and support students in the use of IT.

Ingredients of IT

In modern business organisations the computer has become the most important means of producing information from data, and students need to appreciate that IT is a very simple but invaluable tool. In the notes that follow we highlight the operations involved and relate each to a very simple example – of a college lecturer carrying out data-processing operations in order to administer a college excursion.

CAPTURING DATA involves recording data generated by an event or occurrence (e.g. capturing data from invoices, sales slips, meters, counters, etc.).

Sally Smith pays £5 to her Business Studies tutor Pat Green to pay for a college trip to the House of Commons. Pat records this information on a simple spreadsheet.

VERIFYING DATA refers to checking that data has been recorded/captured accurately (e.g. checking that an instrument is working correctly, or cross-checking someone else's recording procedures).

Later in the week Pat runs through the records to find out who still needs to pay.

CLASSIFYING DATA involves putting different types of data into appropriate sections. For example, the sales of a company could be sorted into the different departments that made the sales.

Pat records the students' names under different headings according to what days they attend the college because a number of them are doing different courses.

SORTING DATA is the placing of data elements into a specified order. For example, an inventory file could be sorted into money value order, or into code number order, etc.

Some of the students have paid all of the £5 while others have only made part payments. After a few days Pat sorts the list with those owing most at the top and those who don't owe anything at the bottom.

SUMMARISING DATA can be used to aggregate data. One way in which this can be done is to total up various figures. (e.g. sales figures) or to draw up balancing figures for a balance sheet. Alternatively, it could be used to reduce data logically to a common form (e.g. by producing a list of all employees who were working on the night shift on a particular day).

Pat uses the spreadsheet to calculate the total paid up to any given date and the total amount to be paid.

CALCULATING USING DATA involves computing various figures in a mathematical sense.

Pat can subtract the total amount paid so far by students from the total amount owing to find out how much remains to be paid.

STORING DATA. This involves transferring data to the appropriate medium (floppy disk, microfilm, etc.).

Pat keeps the spreadsheet and other information relating to the trip on a floppy disk. This disk is kept carefully filed ready for access.

RETRIEVING DATA. This involves calling it up from the place of storage.

It only takes a few seconds for Pat to insert the floppy disk and call up the appropriate records at any time.

REPRODUCING DATA. This is the process of transferring the same data from one medium to another. At a simple level this could involve photocopying material, or calling up data from one screen to another – as with Stock Exchange dealing.

Pat could print off a copy showing students with outstanding payments which can be put on the noticeboard. Alternatively students could call up the records through an electronic mail system that Pat has set up to communicate with students.

COMMUNICATING. This involves transferring data from one place to another. This can take place at any stage in the data-processing cycle. The ultimate aim of information processing is to provide information for the final consumer.

As we have seen in the examples above, there is a wide variety of means by which Pat can communicate with the students.

Using IT in organisations

Clearly the use of IT plays an integral part in supporting many core outcomes. In particular, IT applications will support the following outcomes:

3.3 Gather information for an organisation to evaluate the market
3.5 Develop a basic marketing plan for a product or service
4.2 Audit physical resources in a work area
5.2 Construct and monitor a budget for a business project
5.3 Understand and interpret financial statements
6.1 Audit the human resources of an organisation
7.2 Identify and use communication systems and administrative procedures and systems in organisations
7.3 Assess the applicability of, and where appropriate use, relevant technology in the operation of administrative procedures and systems
7.4 Compare administrative systems of different organisations
8.2 Assess the impact of change and innovation in a designated work area and working environment
8.3 Make and justify recommendations for change in an organisation.

A good starting point for looking at the application of IT in organisations is to look at its use in the college or other organisations with which the students are familiar (see page 153 of *Business and Finance*). Students can be encouraged through assignment work to explore ways in which IT can transform organisations. Useful research work can be carried out looking at how IT is being used in various organisations to transform working patterns and procedures. Perhaps students can make recommendations to particular organisations as to how they would benefit from greater awareness and use of IT.

By working with a 'windows environment' students can integrate a range of applications for their own work, enabling them to produce high-quality documents which can be used in presentations and day-to-day study.

IT support should be built into the blocking arrangement of a BTEC course. Students may require individual assistance in developing further IT capability, depending on the level of their prior learning.

General IT skills

On page 154 of *Business and Finance* we have indicated that all students require general IT capability. Students will need to operate major software applications, including word processing, databases, spreadsheets and desktop publishing. Virtually all employees need some familiarity with IT and its application within a particular working environment:

- Managers need sufficient understanding of the latest developments to spot new business opportunities and to carry out changes.
- Technicians, maintenance and craft workers need to deal with IT components in plants and vehicles of all types.

- Clerical workers have to be familiar with a variety of word-processing, spreadsheet, database and similar applications.
- Professionals need to use specialist IT applications – including 'expert systems' – as an aid to decision making.

Students should be given the opportunity to create a profile of their own developing IT capability. A useful support mechanism is the IT skills checklist which is shown on page 169 of *Business and Finance*. The tutor and learner will need to agree on a starting point of existing learning at the start of the course. It will then be possible to identify steps that can be taken to enhance IT capability as a natural part of the course.

Using appropriate technology

Finally, it is worth bringing in a note of caution about the use of appropriate technology. An organisation that spends too much money on buying the latest technology when it cannot sell sufficient quantities of its products is likely to end up with a lot of redundant machinery. Similarly a student who spends too much time using IT applications as part of an assignment which could be done in five minutes on a simple word-processor may be wasting time.

11 Using a Keywords Approach to Developing Business Terminology

Students progressively build up a range of concepts and terms which give them a fuller understanding of how businesses operate, and of the wider business environment. Keywords help learners to grasp an array of terminology.

Keywords can be kept in a personal Business Directory, or can be a highlighted part of ordinary note-taking.

The recording (and understanding) of keywords should be an on-going part of the course.

Clearly it would not be helpful to encounter too many new words in a given learning session. Also, it is important to bear in mind that the understanding of terms and concepts improves with time, so that new terms take on more substance later. Equally, many ideas and concepts are inherently vague – for example there are many views as to what makes a 'fair distribution of resources', and definitions of 'monopoly' and 'accounting aggregates' change from time to time.

Keywords can also be used to highlight differences between the everyday uses of words and their meanings in a business context (e.g. investment, depreciation, cost).

Building up keywords

The following example illustrates the way in which a tutor can help students to build up a collection of keywords. It is assumed that the tutor will (a) suggest learners look up keywords in a business dictionary, or (b) present students with a pre-prepared keywords sheet, or (c) ask students to write down appropriate definitions given by the tutor. In the example the tutor is introducing some background work about the operation of market economies early on in a BTEC National course.

Case Study – Going cold

In August 1991 many leading British newspapers and magazines ran stories about changing eating habits at breakfast time. A typical presentation included the following.

The nation is going cold on the Great British Breakfast. Fears about cholesterol and salmonella in eggs, as well as time pressures on working wives, are contributing to its demise.

Cereal, tea and toast – with polyunsaturated or low-fat margarine, not butter – are now the breakfast-time norm for two-thirds of us.

On a typical weekday, the sausage, egg and bacon that once fuelled the running of an empire are now eaten by only one in ten. One fifth of 2000 respondents in a market research survey said they had no breakfast at all.

> ***** KEYWORD *****
>
> Market research ... Investigation into the facts about a product, the people who buy it and its competitors. Market research can either be 'desk' research (i.e. consulting secondary sources such as directories, yearbooks, government and other official statistics, reports) or primary research (asking customers and other relevant people directly about their product usage and attitudes).

- *Four out of five people try to eat a healthy diet. Half of those rate health as a particularly important factor, and half lay equal emphasis on enjoying their food.*
- *Around two in every five say they are eating more fresh fruit, vegetables and wholemeal or granary bread for health reasons.*
- *Nearly half of the population uses skimmed milk in preference to ordinary full-cream milk.*
- *Half have cut down on fried food.*
- *Hot buttered toast has become a minority treat. More than half now use a soft margarine as their regular spread.*

The case study provides a useful and helpful means for exploring the way in which markets are in a continual state of flux. The context can be used to explore how the personal choices of learners have altered in recent times and how this has influenced the provision of products in the market. How have **consumers** and **producers** acted in the **marketplace**?

The information above tells us about changes in a number of **interrelated markets**. These markets are concerned with meeting the **needs** of consumers at breakfast time. You can see that as time moves on, so too do the **wants** and needs of consumers. Consumers are able to signal their changing preferences by buying more of some products and less of others. (Learners can be asked to note down which of the breakfast products outlined in the case study became more popular and which less popular. The activity can be extended to other familiar markets.)

Buyers are able to communicate their changing preferences for a product by means of rising **demand**. Producers respond to this signal. In a **market economy** producers will try to anticipate demand. Anticipating demand involves looking into the future to assess what consumer requirements will be. ...

From this Case Study the following keywords can be extracted:

Consumer
  A word used to describe the person who actually uses a product or service, sometimes known as the end-user. For instance, the consumer or end-user of a hamburger is the person who eats it; the consumer or end-user of a pair of jeans is the person who wears them.

Producer
  The person who creates the goods or service. There are many

different producers involved in making most products. Each producer adds value to the final product (e.g. the farmer grows crops, which are transported to the food processor, they are then packed, to be sold by the shop).

Marketplace
A market is a situation in which goods can be bought, sold or exchanged, The essential requirements are buyers, sellers, goods and money.

Interrelated markets
Decisions made in one market affect what happens in another. If I spend some money on bacon I will not be able to spend that money on bread. If I buy less bread I will need less butter to spread on it.

Needs and wants
Our needs are made up of our basic survival kit – food, shelter and clothing. Wants go above and beyond this (e.g. for better clothing, better food, improved housing, video recorders, expensive trainers).

Demand
Wants backed up by money.

Market economy
The wide market place around us in which millions of decisions are made about buying and selling by consumers and producers. Consumers vote with their money and producers try to meet consumer demand by producing goods and services.

12 Helping Students to Learn Through Sharing Information by Card Games

Group work is a very helpful vehicle for learning. Students enjoy working together to share information.

Tutors can devise a number of card games which involve the sharing of information. This is particularly helpful in the area of accounts. You will need to prepare a set of cards giving pieces of information. The cards can then be dealt out among a group of students. The task is for the students to share the information to solve a particular problem in a given time period.

For example, students could work in small groups to prepare the Balance Sheet of Mercury Enterprises as at 31 December 1993. The tutor prepares the following cards (perhaps using half sheets of A5 card)

Freehold premises £90,000	Machinery £12,000
Fixtures and fittings £6000	Motor vehicles £10,000
Stocks £28,000	Debtors £6000
Prepayments £1000	Cash £200
Bank overdraft £2600	Creditors £2400
Accrued costs £200	Taxation payable £2000
Ordinary shares £40,000	Preference shares £40,000
Reserves £30,000	Debentures £36,000

The tutor then shuffles the cards before dealing them to a group of four or five students. (You will need to produce several packs on a word processor.) Students can then be given 20 minutes to work collaboratively to try to create a vertical balance sheet. *They should not lay the cards on the table but they should share the information verbally.* For example, they might start off by saying:

'Who has got assets?'
'Let us start with the fixed assets and then go on to the current assets.'
'Who is going to write it down?'

It is hoped that their solution will look something like Figure 12.15 or Figure 12.20 in *Business and Finance*. The tutor would need to present the correct solution on a clearly set out overhead transparency, which can be worked through a section at a time.

This sort of activity can be replicated with many other accounting exercises for trading accounts, profit and loss accounts and working out break-even points.

Students can share ideas, use the terminology of accounts and work to a time constraint. As with any learning device – it can be overused! However, once you have prepared a set of cards you can use them year after year.

They do take time to prepare, but that is always the case with worthwhile learning activities.

13 Using Overhead Transparencies (OHPs)

In this resource pack we have put together a number of attractive overhead transparencies which will help you to work through the course more effectively. The OHPs support the key areas of the text, and we have provided a set of brief guidelines to accompany each image. The OHPs can be used by you to draw out key areas of content and important concepts. Some of the OHPs provide brief specimen answers to selected Tasks and Case Studies. The OHPs can be used to make some simple teaching points in an attractive and lively fashion. They provide a sense of theatre in any classroom and take some of the attention away from you so that you can concentrate of effective delivery.

The following notes are provided by Alan Morris of Nottingham Polytechnic and relate to the effective use of overhead transparencies.

Advantages of OHPs

Using OHPs you are in control of the situation. You can move on at your own pace and you have a clear direction to follow. A great advantage is that you face the group you are addressing. The overhead projector is light to move and is a simple piece of equipment to operate. You can use an overhead projector without darkening the room. Acetates can be pre-prepared to a high-quality finish, and can be stored easily (perhaps in a series of teaching folders).

Effective use of overhead projections

- Make sure that the platen is clean.
- Check that everyone can see clearly. Have a trial before the session starts, and view the screen from the back of the room. Try to fill as much of the screen as possible with the image.
- Make sure that you have focused the projector (once it is in focus it may not need subsequent adjustments).
- Make sure that the projector is parallel with the screen. If you do not line up the projector with the screen you will get a keystoning effect.

Using Overhead Transparencies (OHPs)

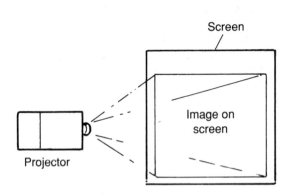

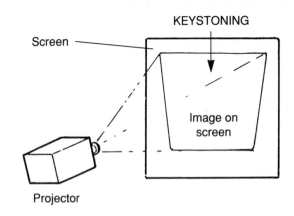

- Check that coloured fringes to your overheads are removed. You can do this by moving a lever at the front of your projector into the correct position. If the lever is too high you will get a brown fringe, too low a blue one. Make sure that you get a clear picture.
- Switch off the projector when you are not using it. If you leave it on you will be left with a distracting noise, and distracting light which will detract from your presentation.

Useful display techniques

There are a number of ways of getting maximum mileage from your OHPs.

Progressive disclosure. Cover up most of the image and gradually unveil successive portions to fit in with your talk.

Overlays. If you are using an OHP which is made up of a number of connecting ingredients (e.g. a diagram showing the circular flow of income) then break up the components into several OHPs that you can lay on top of each other. You can thus build up a total picture from a number of overlays.

Movement. Once you have put an OHP in the correct position, do not move it around. Give the audience plenty of time to look at the image and take in the relevant points – don't swiftly whip it away! A good OHP needs to have a clear theatrical effect, so give it the opportunity to be appreciated in all its glory. Don't put your finger on the platen – any vibration will be magnified. Point to the screen instead!

SECTION 2

Part A – The Working World

The Working World has been designed as a theme to be developed early in a BTEC course. It broaches a range of areas identified from the outcomes which we felt were particularly suitable for young people starting to work for organisations. The aim of the theme is to enable students to understand more about the operations of organisations in general and relate this process to their organisation, and in particular to their role within that organisation. In order to do this we have developed three broad areas within this theme.

Chapter 1 – The Organisation sets out to show that organisations make decisions which affect a variety of different people as well as many other organisations. Such decisions are affected by a range of influences and this chapter briefly explores these influences.

The chapter then looks more specifically at the behaviour of organisations. All organisations have a purpose and pursue specific goals and objectives. In order to achieve these they develop strategies, use tactics and create plans. A crucial decision which all organisations at one stage or another have to take concerns the type of business unit to adopt. This chapter then examines various business units and the developments and changes over recent years.

Chapter 2 – Working for an Organisation makes the reader think about where their place might be within their own organisation. In order for them to identify or appraise a role, they have to examine their organisation's structure. The chapter looks at organisation theories by identifying the need to structure an organisation and, in doing so, examines the division of labour, specialisation and basic management theories. It then looks in detail at organisation structure and design. Frequent references are made to the ways in which many large organisations structure their activities and at the relationships created by such structures.

Chapter 3 – The Needs of the Employee emphasises that effective use of people is a fundamental ingredient in the planning process, and that an organisation's competitive advantage will be determined by its approach to the management of people. An organisation must provide an environment which caters for the individual needs of employees and encourages them to perform well.

This chapter examines organisational cultures and their influence upon employees. It then looks at the basic management and leadership theories and relates these to motivation and rewards.

Chapter 1 The Organisation

Notes for OHPs

OHP 1.1 *What is a good business?*
This OHP refers to page 3 of the text. Students could be advised to think about the ingredients of a good business. This could be set as a task in which students work over a 15 minute time span in groups of two or three. The OHP could then be used to follow up the task. The three statements below the chart emphasise that a good business will adopt a broad approach to its activities by not becoming short-termist and through endeavouring to become a good citizen.

OHP 1.2 *Making dog biscuits*
This OHP is designed to follow up the dog biscuit Case Study on pages 4 and 5. It provides the answers to questions 1–10. (NB There are 1000 kg in a tonne.)

OHP 1.3 *Which way forward?*
This refers to page 16 of the text. Emphasis in this OHP should be placed upon the action required to achieve goals. Such action will require developing a strategy over a long period using a long-term plan, and of providing the mechanism through which tactical decisions may take place. Various business goals are indicated beneath the chart. It might be worth asking students which of the goals they feel to be the most important, and why.

OHP 1.4 *Types of business organisation*
This is a straightforward OHP, extracted from page 19, which distinguishes between private and public sector organisations.

OHP 1.5 *Privatisation*
This OHP is designed to emphasise the arguments both for and against privatisation which appear on page 26 of the text.

Responses to selected Tasks and Case Studies

TASK – Opportunity cost (page 2)

1 Although Jill makes £125 for the day by giving a talk at a school, she has to consider how much she would otherwise earn from illustrating on that day, as well as the cost of any commissions she might lose through not being immediately available.
2 On the one hand the boat builders are improving their profit, but they are refusing work to meet the orders. Although the job may lead to a larger order, if it doesn't, they may experience difficulty re-establishing their core business.
3 John will be £60 better off but will have to weigh this gain against the leisure activities he may have to forfeit.

CASE STUDY – Chip vending (page 3)

This is intended as an inductive study to make students think carefully about how organisations operate. We would expect students to use common sense to show how the case was turned into a successful proposition.

1 Answers might vary widely. They might refer to consumer needs, time of the day, quality of chips, etc.
2 a Answers may involve setting up a company, employing people, choosing a name, finding somewhere to locate.
  b A range of sources (relatives, friends, bank etc.)
  c Records, offices, etc.
  d Taking the idea further, researching the market, follow-up ideas, etc.
  e They have to include more people in their idea – staff, providers of finance, managers, etc.
  f Correspondence, accounting information, stocks, etc.
3 This is designed to encourage students to think about what else would be necessary to turn a good idea into a business. Their answers might include further ideas, premises, managerial skills, the right business environment.

CASE STUDY – Weaknesses of a planned economy (page 12)

1. No.
2. Answers may include: inefficient; lacks competition; badly organised; does not cater for needs; bureaucratic; encourages black market.
3. Black market.
4. The writer suggests the abolition of coupons, the increasing of prices and the movement towards a less centralised system.
5. Suggestions might vary widely but could include further competition, abolition of price-fixing, less centralised control.
6. Many problems have been encountered in changing this system. Indeed the problems themselves are changing all of the time! Answers will vary widely but may include: shortages; unemployment; inefficiency; effects on incomes; standards of living.

TASKS – page 13

1.
   a planning official
   b planning official
   c private citizen
   d planning official/private citizen
   e planning official
   f private citizen
   g planning official/private citizen
   h planning official
   i private citizen
   j private citizen.
2.
   a planning official/private entrepreneur
   b planning official
   c planning official
   d planning official
   e planning official
   f planning official
   g private entrepreneur.
3. Answers will vary and may be used to form the basis of discussion.

TASK – page 18

a £20.50
b £5.50
c 70 pence.

TASK – page 23

a Advantages of franchising for the franchisor include: easy to expand and develop brand; increases income potential; allows economies of scale to be obtained.
b Advantages of franchising for the franchisee include: trading under a well-known name; using an idea with a proven track-record; may provide a local monopoly.

CASE STUDY – Making railways more competitive (pages 27/28)

1. Regulation – control and responsibility for. Privatisation – movement from public to private ownership. Competition – other organisations competing for the same customers. Monopoly – one organisation acting as sole supplier of a good or service. Discipline of the private sector – having to compete to survive and make profits to satisfy shareholders.
2. Benefits will include: new powers of regulation; commitments to quality; new means of dealing with complaints; 'chartermark' for high standards of service; compensation rules.
3. New costs might include cost of paperwork, compensation costs, renewal of tickets.
4. Both will be difficult to measure.
5. Some may construe this as a political issue or a PR measure. Many may feel that more money should be spent upon the service. Others may welcome ideas but feel that they have come too late.
6. This may contain any reasoned and supported argument.
7. These may include: to provide public investment; because other railways are subsidised; to provide an integrated transport infrastructure; services benefit communities; keeps traffic from roads.

CASE STUDY – Marks & Spencer knickers (pages 28/29)

1. Factors might include: wide availability, price, reputation, quality.
2. The cost advantage is dependent on maintaining volume, which provides economies of scale, and provides them with a gross margin of 40 per cent on a sales volume of £500 million.
3. Economies of scale reduce unit costs over a larger output. They might provide technological, commercial, managerial and financial advantages. (see pages 339 – 340).
4. Small firms would have to go for larger margins over smaller production runs. They would not, therefore, be able to compete on price.
5. Such factors should be wide-ranging and might include: further opportunities in Europe and their impressive reputation and quality.
6. Threats to M&S's knicker sales might come from European competition, other firms becoming larger and developing similar economies, recession and its effect upon high street sales, etc.
7. They may measure success by looking at sales in value and volume, using comparisons with previous years, comparing with forecasts, seeing if successes match objectives, etc.

CASE STUDY – Changes in the coal industry (pages 29/30)

1. The information indicates that it is targeted for privatisation; its biggest threat is from loss of business from the electricity suppliers; its coal is expensive and the sulphur content is high.
2. Slimming down will get rid of the least profitable parts, improve overall productivity and make its product more attractive.
3. This will depend on the views of various members of the group and will provide a useful discussion topic.
4. Privatisation may make the industry more competitive, improve efficiency, make it responsible to a wide base of shareholders and make the industry more profitable.
5. The privatised industry will be substantially smaller, more efficient and more profitable.
6. They will have to be more competitive and possibly more ruthless. We will probably see more price discrimination as well as many public relations activities.

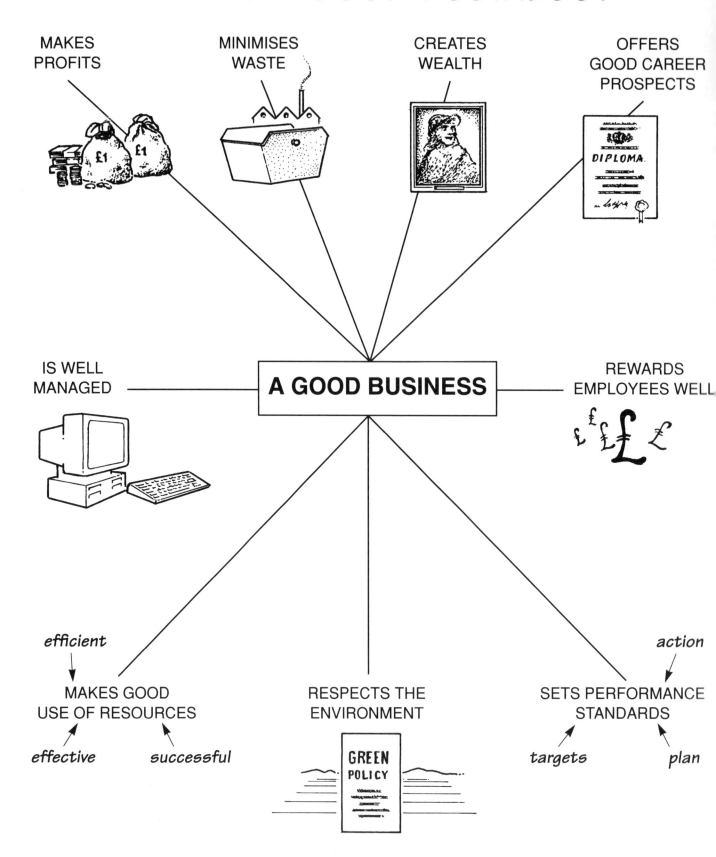

OHP 1.2

MAKING DOG BISCUITS

1. Ingredients cost the most.

2. Maintaining buildings and machinery, heating and lighting.

3. £126,500

4. Suggestions may include: – buying cheaper ingredients
   – economising on energy
   – employing fewer staff
   – spending less on packaging, etc.

5. £718,750

6. £228.65

7. 2,875,000 boxes

8. Yes, Total income = £2,875,000 – 2,629,475

9. £1.10 = £533,025
   £1.25 = £964,275
   £1.40 = £1,395,525

10. Contents, ingredients, quality, size, features, etc.

WHICH WAY FORWARD?

Goals might include:
- profit
- market share
- growth
- satisficing
- steady income
- freedom of expression

OHP 1.4

TYPES OF BUSINESS ORGANISATION

Private sector businesses are owned by PRIVATE INDIVIDUALS and GROUPS. The main types are:

Type of enterprise	Who owns the business?	Who controls the business?	Usual sources of finance
Sole trader	One person	One person	Owner's savings, bank loans or overdraft, profits
Partnership	Two or more partners	The partners	Partners' savings, bank loans or overdraft, profits
Company	Two or more shareholders	The directors	Share issues, bank loans or overdraft, venture capital, profits
Co-operative	Two or more members	Managers and other co-operators jointly	Share issues, bank loans or overdraft, profits

Limited liability protects shareholders if a company is unable to meet its debts. Shareholders will not be liable to lose their personal possessions to pay the money owed.

Public sector businesses are owned by the STATE. They include:

        Local government enterprises

        Central government enterprises

PRIVATISATION

Arguments in favour:

(i) State-run firms lack efficiency.

(ii) It widens share ownership.

(iii) It makes industries more competitive.

(iv) Privatised companies will provide a better service.

(v) Money from sale can be used to lower taxes.

Arguments against:

(i) Some industries should be owned by the community.

(ii) Can lead to price rises.

(iii) Industries may cut services to make profits.

(iv) Money raised only cuts taxes of better off.

(v) Competition duplicates use of resources.

Chapter 2 Working for an Organisation

Notes for OHPs

OHP 2.1 *Specialisation*
This OHP refers to pages 32 and 33 of the text. Specialisation can take place in a variety of ways. The purpose of this OHP is to emphasise the different types of specialisation. One Task encourages students to think about the different types of specialisation in their college or place of work. Their conclusions can be used as a basis for discussion. The area can then be developed further by asking them:
- why organisations specialise
- what the advantages and disadvantages of specialisation may be.

OHP 2.2 *The Prime Minister's role and Fayol's fourteen functions*
This OHP refers to question 2 of the Case Study 'Finding a job for the Prime Minister' which appears on page 35. It may be used by the tutor to lead students through the results of their analysis. Responses may vary widely but could include:

1. Division of work – into government departments and ministerial responsibilities.
2. Authority and responsibility – vested in PM who has widespread authority and is responsible to the electorate.
3. Discipline – has the power to hire and fire.
4. Unity of command – PM makes decisions and takes responsibility for the decisions of others.
5. Unity of direction – follows party policies.
6. Subordination of individual interest to group interest – electorate and party come first.
7. Remuneration – PM is in a paid post.
8. Centralisation – delegation of authority to ministerial departments.
9. Chain of authority – by nature of post, department and responsibilities.
10. Order – cabinet ministers will generally have a title and some form of job description.
11. Equity – this may be dependent on how the PM is seen to treat ministers. John Major's approach seems to be clearly different from that of his predecessor!
12. Stability of tenure – normally for five years unless an election is called earlier or unless the party members reject leadership.
13. Initiative – very important role for PM. Try to emphasise the role of strategic thinking and of planning ahead.
14. Esprit de corps – the PM should try to make the Cabinet work together as a governmental team.

OHP 2.3 *Division by function*
This refers to pages 37 – 39 of the text. It may be used to introduce division by function and to briefly go through the operations of the various types of department.

OHP 2.4 *Division by process*
On page 41 is a short example of division by process of a manufacturer of chicken nuggets. This OHP visually expands this with a diagram showing the various stages of manufacture of pizzas. Students could be asked:
- why divide by process?
- what are the benefits?

OHP 2.5 *Matrix structure*
This is a copy of the diagram appearing on page 44. It is intended to help with the description of the workings of a matrix.

Responses to selected Tasks and Case Studies

CASE STUDY – Anglia motorbikes (pages 33/34)

This is a straightforward case designed to reinforce the benefits of specialisation with a reference to a simple fictitious example. The Case Study also enables students to use numerical skills to analyse a situation.

1. Specialisation seems to have affected Anglia's:
   a. *employees*
      - With an increase in days lost to industrial disputes from 18 to 1420 (7789 per cent increase)
      - With an increase in sickness from 1245 days to 3460 days (178 per cent increase).
   b. *management*
      It will be easier for managers to administer the fewer models produced. Managers may also be able to specialise in particular processes or disciplines. However, their jobs may be made more difficult with disputes and absenteeism. (NB If workers become too specialised it may be difficult to cover for them when absent.)
   c. *shareholders*
      Specialisation has increased profitability.
   d. *customers*
      They will have limited choice and products will not be hand-built. Although prices may fall, some may feel that an era has ended.
2. Students will come up with a range of ideas. It might even be worth them briefly discussing Anglia's plight in groups. They may suggest trying to cut costs, the increasing of prices, only partially modernising, that the heritage should be emphasised, etc.

TASK – page 39

Marketing is essentially a strategic function responsible for satisfying consumer requirements profitably. It will involve knowledge of consumers and the environment in which they operate, as well as market research, planning, the mix etc. Selling is part of the promotional area of the marketing mix. Its priority is in getting orders for goods.

TASK – page 39

The events of 1991 might have affected a personnel department in a variety of different ways. For example, making redundancies, having to reassure employees about poor industrial performance, encouraging employees to accept low wage claims and thus improve competitiveness, fewer jobs advertised, larger number of applications for such posts, general uncertainty.

Section 2 – The Working World

CASE STUDY – The Bank of England (pages 39/40)

1. Dividing by function is necessary because the Bank has clearly defined and separated functions, because certain functions are carried out in different places, and as functions will probably require different types of staffing skills.
2. Benefits of dividing by function in this instance might include: a concentration of people working on similar projects in the same area; the development of subject expertise; easy to understand.
3. This question is designed to make students think about an employee's information requirements in the workplace For example, it could be argued that all employees should understand how their organisation is divided. This may improve their motivation, make them aware of opportunities, help them to understand how their role fits into the organisation, and help them to understand the policies, activities and overall direction of the organisation.

CASE STUDY – Hanson PLC (pages 40/41)

1. Hanson structures by product group (e.g. consumer, building, industrial).
2. A conglomerate, by its very nature, will produce a diversity of products. Division by product is the most logical and sensible way of dividing such an organisation.

CASE STUDY – Yorkshire Water (pages 42/43)

1. Water is expensive to transport and supplies are, therefore, more often than not, localised. Although some technical services may be available across a number of areas, it would seem appropriate for each area to take responsibility for its own supplies.
2. Advantages may include: each unit becomes responsive to each local environment; it caters for local needs; it is easy to understand.

   Disadvantages may include: an organisation may become fragmented with too many different policies for too many different areas; if areas are too small they may not gain economies of scale or be able to benefit from specialisation; they may become difficult to coordinate.

CASE STUDY – Delegation and decentralisation (page 45)

1. Phil's situation helps to emphasise delegation and Sally's situation illustrates decentralisation.
2. The dangers of too much delegation might include: an employee might feel that they require more freedom; they are being told to do something without being allowed to think for themselves; their actions lack flexibility and responsibility.

   The dangers of too much decentralisation might include: some employees do not like to take responsibility; it might put them under pressure; they might prefer more guidance and help.

TASK – page 46

Advantages of putting names and pictures on a chart include: employees get to know who to deal with; it is a personal touch; it indicates that people are important, not just the post they hold.

Disadvantages include: having to update it when people leave or change posts; the expense; there may be too much information to put on to such a chart.

TASK – page 47

It is possible for a functional specialist to provide advice which conflicts with the actions of a line manager. for example, a marketing department may request the halting of a production run to meet a small order, and this may conflict with the advice given by an operations manager to produce in large batches.

CASE STUDY – Yorkshire Bank PLC (page 48)

1. Yorkshire Bank is divided up by function.
2. This is difficult as the chart refers to functions rather than employees, but it would seem to indicate a tall structure.
3. Lateral relationships might include relationships between teams comprising employees from each of the group services divisions. It would also involve the decisions made by general managers of each division when they meet. Any of the group services provides a function relationship. Line relationships would move downwards from the senior posts.
4. It enables them to know more about different parts of the organisation and how they relate to each other. It provides them with an idea of wider opportunities. It is a useful source of internal information.
5. Organisation charts tend to have more width than depth.

CASE STUDY – Eight-freight Ltd (pages 49/50)

1
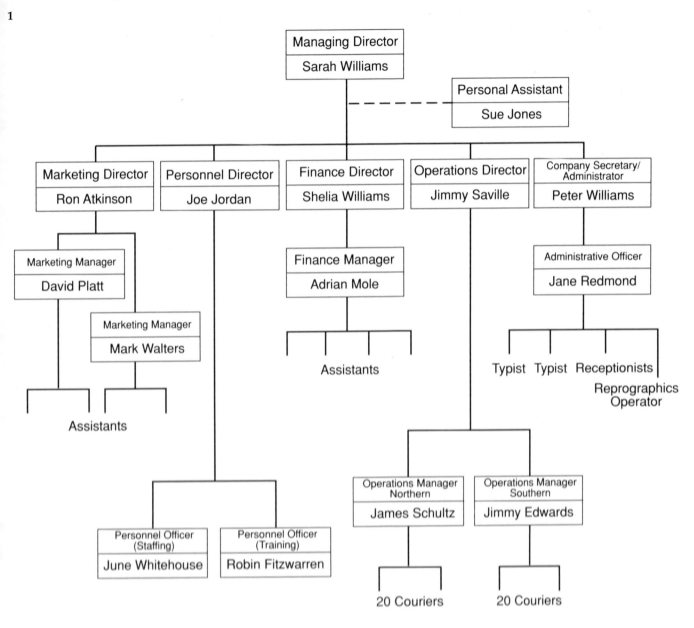

2 It is divided by function according to departments. Operations are further divided geographically.

3 Any reasonable answer which develops practical comments – such as to foster loyalties and generate team spirit – should be encouraged.

OHP 2.1

SPECIALISATION

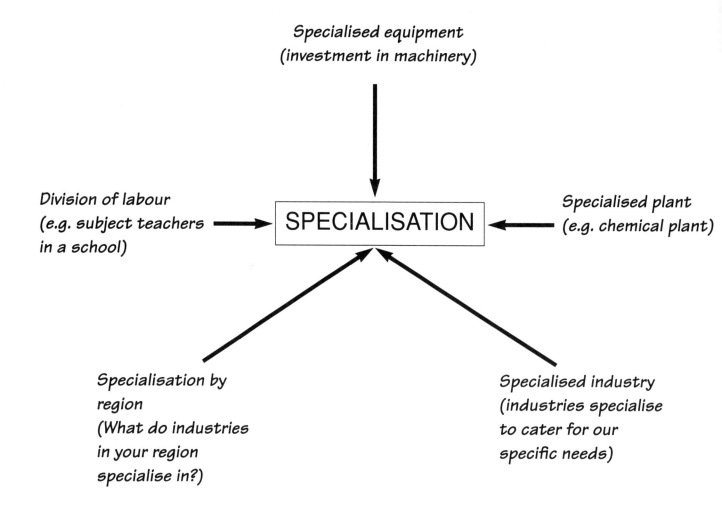

TASK
Identify the various types of specialisation either in the college you attend or in your place of work. Discuss your conclusions.

THE PRIME MINISTER'S ROLE AND FAYOL'S FOURTEEN PRINCIPLES

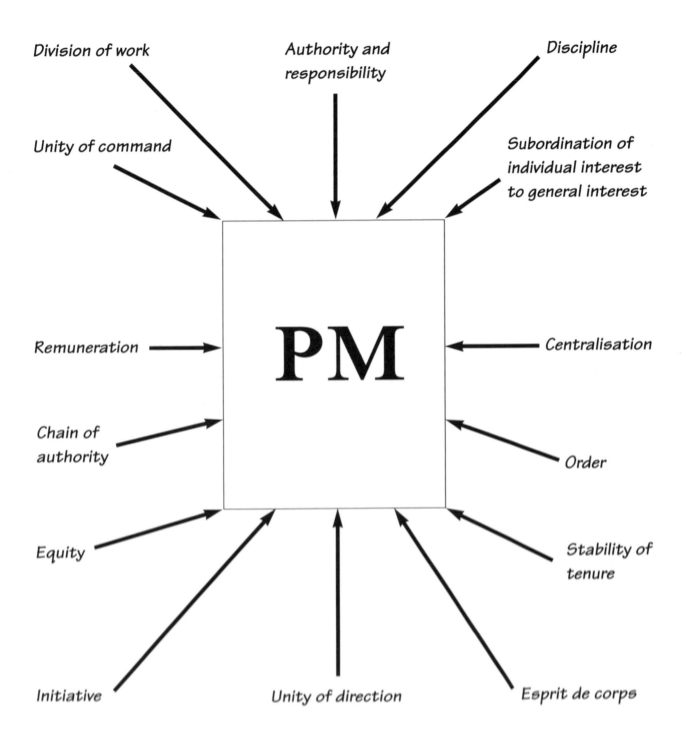

DIVISION BY FUNCTION

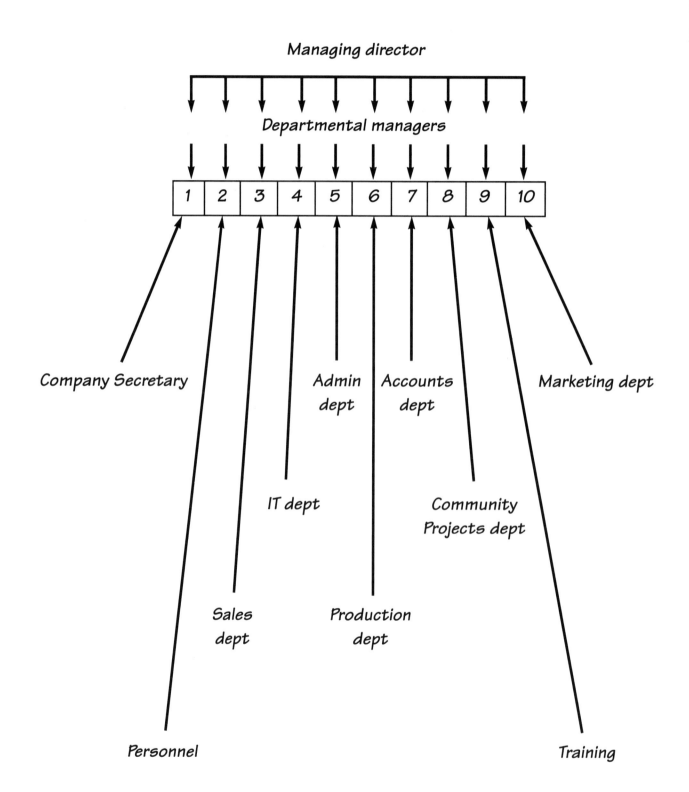

DIVISION BY PROCESS
(PIZZA MANUFACTURE)

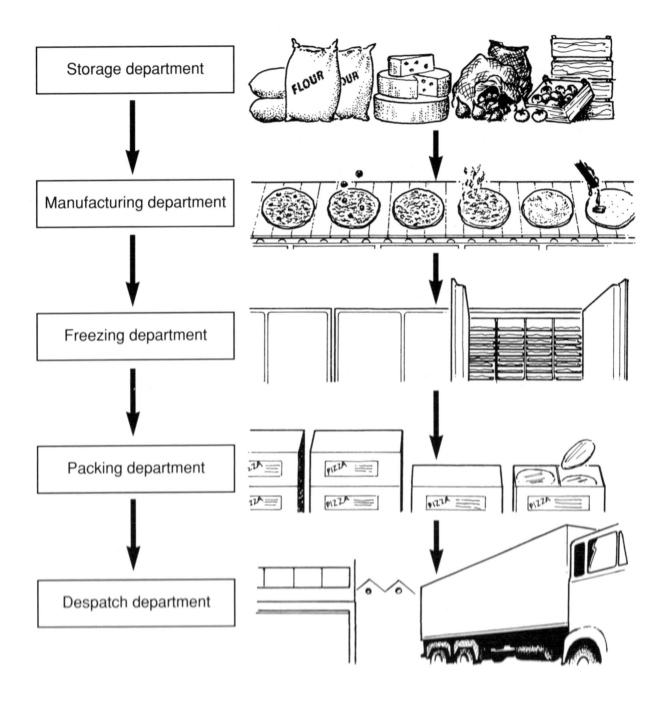

OHP 2.5

MATRIX STRUCTURE

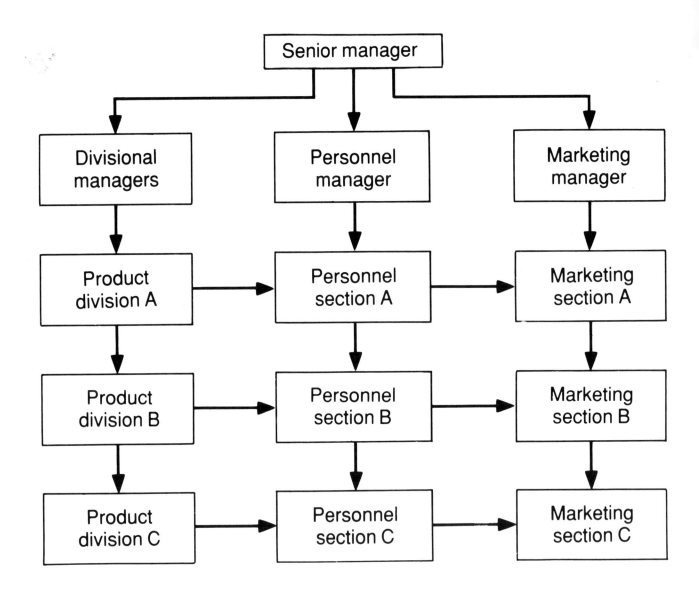

Chapter 3 The Needs of the Employee

Notes for OHPs

OHP 3.1 *Types of organisational culture*
Understanding cultures helps students to appreciate how organisations operate as well as how people are treated within each organisation. Though some organisations do not fit neatly into a particular category, there are four broad areas into which most organisations fall or within which their activities can be identified. This OHP refers to work covered from pages 52 to 55 in the text. Each of the four cultures is illustrated by reference to a diagram and these are shown on the OHP. Such diagrams can be used to introduce each different culture to students.

OHP 3.2 *Trait theories of leadership*
This OHP refers to the trait theories of leadership which appear on pages 57 and 58 of the text. Trait theories deal with the personal characteristics of the leader. Such characteristics would be very important when leading a party on an outdoor excursion! On this OHP the 15 traits from an American study are identified and then related to a practical situation. The question below the illustration may be used to form the basis of a discussion.

OHP 3.3 *Continuum of leadership styles/The managerial grid*
This OHP deals with commonly used illustrations from two style theories of managerial leadership. The continuum of leadership styles from the work of Tannenbaum and Schmidt – see page 59 of text – reflects upon the authoritarian versus democratic issue. The managerial grid, from page 60, refers to concern for people against the concern for production. The diagrams help the user to identify the particular management leadership style to which they are subject and are very useful for discussing examples such as those shown in the text on page 60.

OHP 3.4 *Maslow's hierarchy of human needs*
Maslow's hierarchy of human needs and its relevance to motivation appears on page 62 of the text. The OHP is designed to help the user to illustrate the level of needs which each wishes to satisfy before moving on to a higher level.

OHP 3.5 *Monetary and other rewards*
This refers to the area covered from page 65 to page 66 of the text. It explains what monetary and non-monetary rewards are intended to achieve and relates this to the need for some form of job evaluation.

Responses to selected Tasks and Case Studies

CASE STUDY – comparing two organisations (page 52)

1 Advantages of working for Organisation A might include: employees may feel that their contribution is valued; they are encouraged to make decisions; they work together as part of a team.
   Disadvantages of working for Organisation A might include: some employees may not wish to contribute ideas; such flexibility may put them under pressure; they may prefer to work in a more rigidly structured situation.
   Advantages of working for Organisation B might include: employees know precisely where they stand; working life is predictable and secure; they know what they can and cannot do; everybody is easily recognised by job title and description.
   Disadvantages of working for Organisation B might include: employees may feel frustrated because they are not being consulted; they may feel that they have few opportunities to utilise potential; too much formality creates too many barriers.
2 This is an opportunity for students to think about the sort of organisation they would like to work within and the reasons for this.
3 Organisations differ so widely because they are dependent on people and people differ so widely. Other influences which determine why organisations differ may include: the type of market the organisations is in; the organisation's background and history; the general environment of the organisation; the goals of the organisation; the way it is structured.

CASE STUDY – Apricot Computers (page 53)

1 It was Roger Foster's managerial skills such as energy, drive, vision and overall business acumen which created and developed Apricot in its earlier years. Without such leadership Apricot would probably not have achieved many of its later successes.
2 As organisations grow larger they become more difficult to control. There is also a feeling of lack of challenge, and managers may be frustrated because they lack the power to make decisions.
3 Advantages may include: stability; subject to strong leadership; decisions are made for you.
   Disadvantages may include: feeling of frustration; lack of participation or consultation; lack of challenge; low morale.

TASK – page 54

In a role culture an employee benefits from security and predictability.

CASE STUDY – Introducing the matrix into colleges (page 54)

1 In a matrix more posts are created, employees are frequently asked to work in teams, expertise is recognised, and new posts are constantly being made available.
2 There are few clearly defined strands of formal authority, employees may lack direction, coordination may be difficult, and the matrix may create confusion.

CASE STUDY – Two contrasting styles (page 58)

1 Paul Judge comes across as being more Theory Y than Theory X. The case indicates that he is clearly concerned for people as well as production.
   Sir Peter Walters seems to be a Theory X manager who leads strongly. The case seems to indicate that he is autocratic and would be concerned for production rather than people.
2 Each style may be effective in its own way and be particularly appropriate for different situations.

Section 2 – The Working World

CASE STUDY – A British cure for a German company (page 61)

1 The Bavarian lift-truck maker had suffered poor trading results and required contingency leadership appropriate to such a situation. It led to short-term action such as reduction in capacity and then a longer-term strategy which has doubled market-share.

2 It is difficult to say from the facts, but probably not. Some answers might contain alternative suggestions which may provide the basis for discussion.

CASE STUDY – Understanding managerial commitment (page 62)

1 Managers may have lacked motivation because they themselves felt they were not being led, their work was too flexible, 'standing on their own two feet' created stressful situations and, as a result, they felt they were not being rewarded for taking on such responsibility.

2 Answers to this question might refer to any form of monetary or non-monetary reward or refer to realistic ideas which could be used to improve motivation.

CASE STUDY – Why industry thrives on the carrot (page 67)

1 Advantages may include: improvements in productivity; quality and service.

2 Answers for this may vary. It would be interesting to compare the reasons for such answers.

3 Recognition helps individuals to feel that their efforts have been valued. It may be particularly appropriate in an organisation with large numbers of staff. The second part of this question may prompt a variety of practical suggestions.

4 This question may be used as the basis for discussion. It might be worth students working in groups to consider further ideas for motivating employees.

Supporting Notes for Part A – The Working World

Further areas to explore

It is possible to develop further some of the work from this section. For example, in the first chapter we look at goals and objectives. An area which links in to this and which lends itself to student research is 'the mission statement'. You might wish to ask students to find a local organisation with a mission statement. They could then establish how such a statement links with the organisation's objectives and find out what it is intended to do for the morale of those people who come across it. In this way students will link more closely the work of the first chapter (The Organisation) with that of the third (The Needs of the Employee).

Another area which could be explored further is the different types of organisational structure. Students could be asked to conduct a survey of part of your local environment which they know well. They could identify different structures and make comparisons between them. You could also ask them to choose one of the organisations and write off for a copy of its organisation chart. (NB It is usually sensible to contact an organisation beforehand if a large number of students are likely to use them. One of the authors was recently 'ticked off' by a senior local government officer for writing an assignment which started an assault on the Town Hall!)

Another feature of this section is that it lends itself to analysing management theory further. It could be possible to develop the leadership work in Chapter 3 by introducing 'management by objectives'.

Assignment ideas and suggestions

The essential feature of this section is 'the organisation', finding out how it may be structured and what it might be like as an employer. This lends itself easily to an assignment based either on a visit to an organisation, or on an outside speaker visiting the place of study. Students can be asked to find out about the organisation, its development, its structure, how it functions, its culture, the type of leadership, motivation etc. They are then made responsible for their own learning process. When the visit takes place or the speaker comes in, students will be placed in a situation whereby they have to ask questions to find out what they want to know. This can be a very effective form of learning activity.

Any assignment which helps students to understand the basic ingredients of a small business may be useful at an early stage in this area. (NB *Business Studies Investigations* published by the Shell Education Service and written by Rob Dransfield may provide a useful source of case study materials which lend themselves for adaptation for assignment purposes. Another useful source of material for assignments is the *Single Market News* published by the DTI: there are several case studies towards the end of the magazine which could be adapted and developed for assignment use.)

'Motivation' can be a difficult area to develop an assignment around. The more obvious questions a student would probably want to ask are sometimes the questions they should not ask (e.g. about pay)! Perhaps the best way to develop this area is to look very generally at how an organisation attempts to motivate its workforce. Though in the past it was rare for organisations to divulge much information, today many businesses are more than happy to tell you how they value their people. Nissan in Washington and Rothmans in Darlington are two prime examples. Information packs from various organisations may help you to create an assignment. It helps if an assignment refers to an organisation known to your students.

TYPES OF ORGANISATIONAL CULTURE

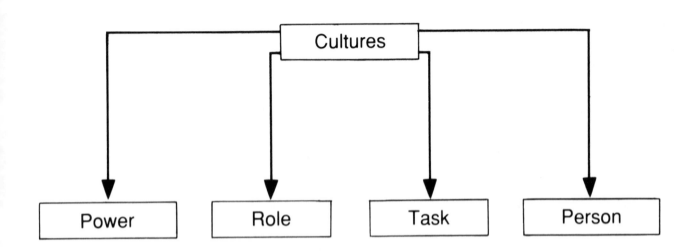

POWER

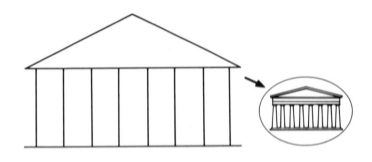

ROLE

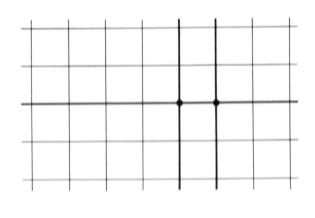

TASK

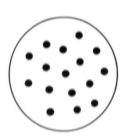

PERSON

OHP 3.2

TRAIT THEORIES OF LEADERSHIP

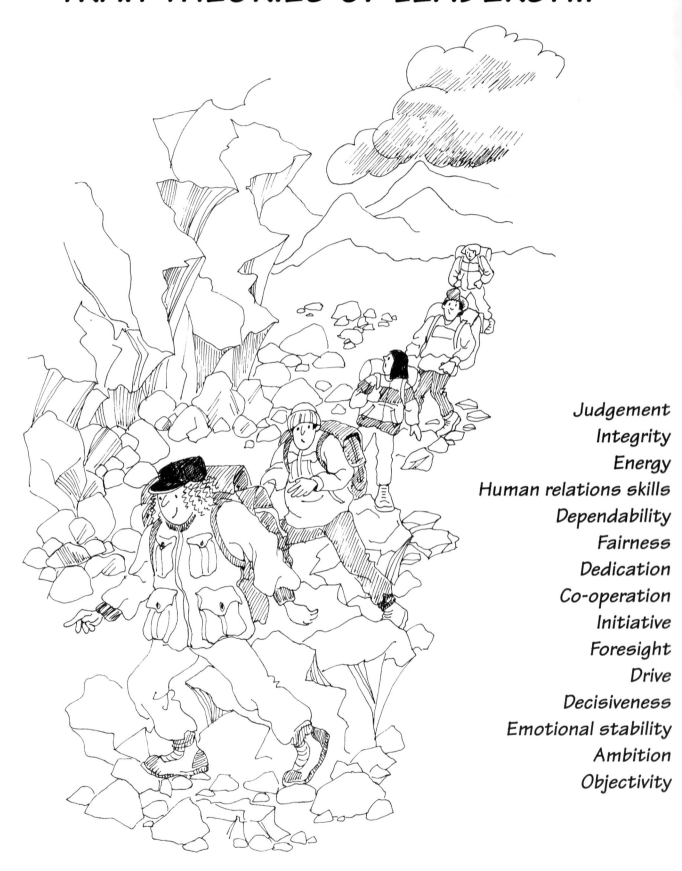

Judgement
Integrity
Energy
Human relations skills
Dependability
Fairness
Dedication
Co-operation
Initiative
Foresight
Drive
Decisiveness
Emotional stability
Ambition
Objectivity

How might these traits be useful in the above situation?

CONTINUUM OF LEADERSHIP STYLES

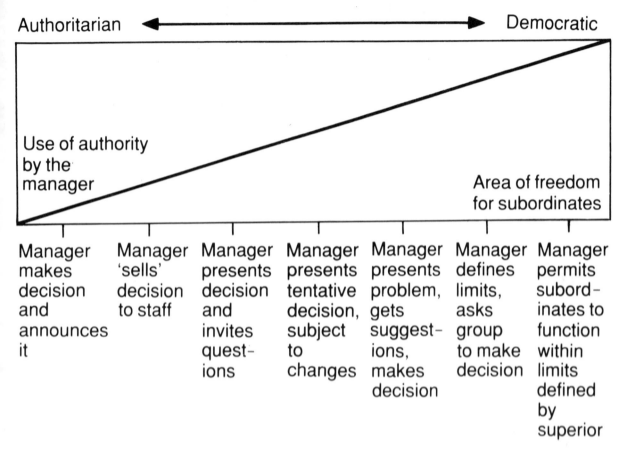

THE MANAGERIAL GRID

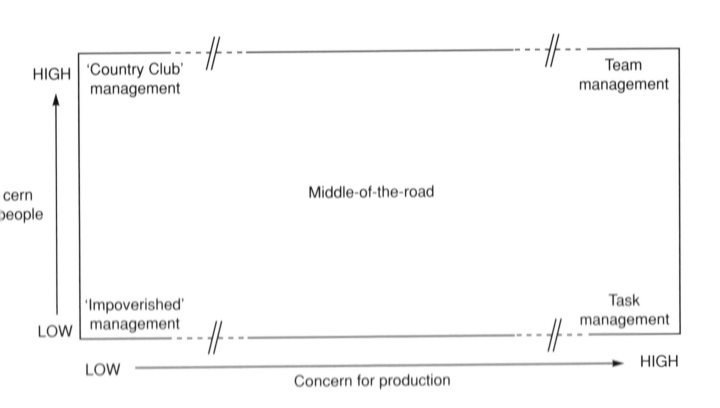

MASLOW'S HIERARCHY OF HUMAN NEEDS

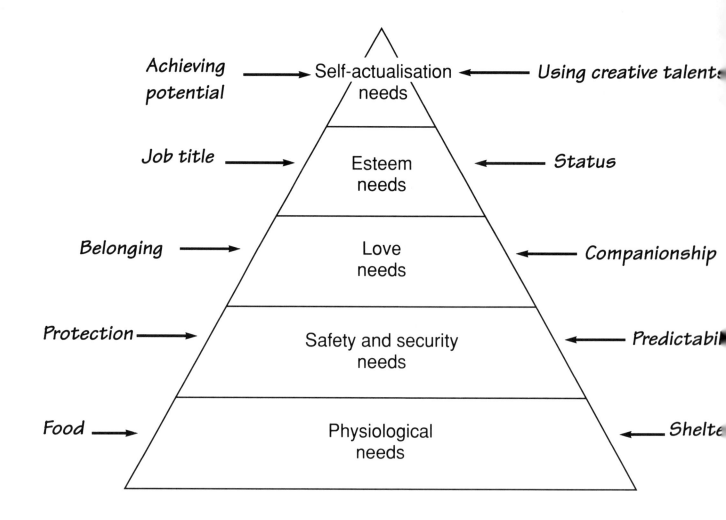

MONETARY AND OTHER REWARDS

Monetary and non-monetary rewards should be designed to attract, maintain and motivate employees

The policy of rewards should:
- *ensure that the organisation can recruit both the quality and quantity of staff it requires*
- *foster staff loyalty*
- *provide rewards for good performance as well as incentives.*

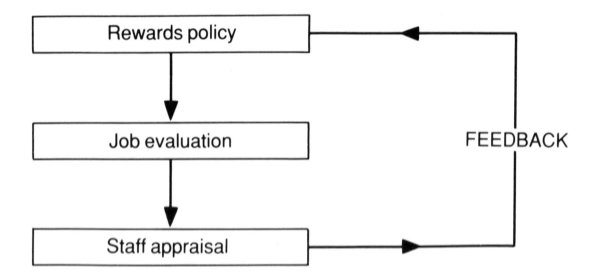

Job evaluation aims to:
- *establish a rank order of jobs*
- *evaluate the differences and put them into an appropriate pay structure*
- *ensure that judgements about jobs are made on objective grounds.*

SECTION 2

Part B – The Client

Today we live in the age of the consumer; power has shifted from the seller to the buyer. The emphasis in this section is on marketing. In order to achieve the organisational objectives which were outlined in Chapter 1, an organisation must discover what existing and potential customers or clients want. Doing this enables it to pursue its objectives profitably.

Marketing must not be taught as a static process. Its success rests upon how well the organisation can respond to the dynamics of the marketplace where forces are changing all the time. As a result this section is about both planning for action and taking action. The strategic element of marketing involves matching long-term marketing objectives with organisational objectives and then using short-term tactical decisions to meet changing circumstances. Such tactical decisions provide greater flexibility. Developing an effective marketing plan involves elements of the marketing mix and, if the plan is effective, consumers will be satisfied and the objectives of the organisation will be met.

Chapter 4 – Assessing Customer Needs analyses the importance of the customer and the need for marketing. Marketing is then defined. The chapter looks at elements in customer behaviour which are important for the marketer, including techniques for dividing customers into different groups – such as social stratification. Market research techniques are assessed in detail and simple methods of analysing and presenting data are suggested.

Chapter 5 – The Market-place sets out some of the key principles underlying any market. In particular, it looks at the interaction of demand and supply and at the importance of elasticity. It then relates this to marketing planning and the marketing process by using case analysis.

Chapter 6 – Marketing Products and Services deals with the practical aspects of marketing activities. Information from market research as well as an understanding of customer behaviour enables an organisation to segment its market. Segmentation allows positioning to take place. Having decided on a strategy an organisation can start to use the marketing mix. This chapter analyses each element of the mix in detail. It then considers how each could be used, and relates their use to the various phases of the product life-cycle.

Chapter 4 Assessing Customer Needs

Notes for OHPs

OHP 4.1 *The marketing process*
This OHP can be used when looking at the definition of marketing which appears on page 70 of the text. The process may be viewed as a circular flow. Marketing enables consumer needs to be anticipated, identified and fulfilled profitably. Some of these profits may be reinvested into further marketing activities which can generate more profits.

OHP 4.2 *The steps in a marketing plan*
This OHP is intended to emphasise that marketing is a process of planning. Each step could represent a plan. The fulfilment of each plan will make an organisation more profitable. The OHP also makes the distinction between marketing strategy and marketing tactics.

OHP 4.3 *Understanding customer behaviour*
This OHP distinguishes between types of customers, from page 71 of the text. It then goes further to indicate the various influences upon consumers from pages 71 to 74 and the factors influencing organisational behaviour from pages 74 to 75.

OHP 4.4 *Market research*
This OHP refers to page 76 of the text. It can be used to introduce market research and highlight the various parts of the definition.

OHP 4.5 *The questionnaire*
This OHP is designed to make students think carefully about questionnaire construction and refers to pages 81 and 82 of the text.

Responses to selected Tasks and Case Studies

CASE STUDY – What do customers really want? (page 70)

1 By researching his market he identified that consumers wanted something different.
2 He looked at an industry which was mature, had a relatively dowdy image and in which all of the products or services were relatively similar. Innovative marketing in this context means that he felt that a lot of consumers wanted something totally different and that he could match his revolutionary ideas with their requirements.

CASE STUDY – Party, party, party (page 71)

1 Ideas for reaching this particular type of consumer may vary widely. Students may mention professional journals, private sportscentres, clubs or groups, up-market magazines, etc.
2 Students will probably automatically identify young people and their ideas should be encouraged. It would be possible to get them to take their ideas further by looking in detail at specific groups of people, preparing a questionnaire and undertaking a research activity.

TASK – page 72

Students may come up with a range of goods or services. For example:
- *Physiological* needs would include basic items such as a coat or a pair of shoes.
- *Safety and security* needs might be locks on a front door or a seat belt in the car.
- *Love* needs might include a bunch of flowers, a pint in the pub or membership fees of a club.
- *Esteem* needs might provide a particular make of car or type of clothing worn.
- *Self-actualisation* needs might include the desire for further education or a trip to an unusual place.

Assessing Customer Needs

CASE STUDY – Launching new products (page 74)

1. Cadbury's 'Strollers' – The product is intended for the adult leisure market, perhaps to be eaten at home while undertaking a leisure activity and to be viewed as something different from the present-day range of savoury products. As far as the economic determinants of consumer demand are concerned, it will appeal to changing tastes and may be regarded as better value for money than some substitute products. It would probably appeal to the love and esteem needs of a fairly up-market consumer in category C1 upwards with an affluent lifestyle.
Boddington's Draughtflow – This is clearly designed for the more discerning beer drinker. As a premium product its success may be determined by incomes, tastes and the prices of substitute products. It may appeal to love, esteem and possible self-actualisation needs of a C1 upwards beer drinker who likes to be seen to appreciate the good things in life.
Pepsi-Cola six-bottle crate – This is probably aimed at the family market to encourage people to become regular cola drinkers, and to increase depth of market penetration. Its demand may be determined by taste, the actions of other producers – Coke – and possibly consumer incomes. It will appeal to the love needs of C1s and C2s who will drink cola as part of their lifestyle.
Cafetino coffee drink – This is quite a revolutionary idea in a fully mature market. Its success will be determined by incomes and fashions. It may appeal to esteem or even self-actualisation needs of C1s, Bs and As. It may also symbolise an affluent lifestyle.
Alfa Romeo Cloverleaf – The product is up-market and very different from other products in the market. Its success will be determined by tastes and (particularly) incomes. It will be directed at the esteem needs of As and Bs with an expensive lifestyle.

2. The economic determinants of consumer demand will determine how well the product is received and the size of market which develops. Appeal to motivation will help producers to develop the product around the needs of potential consumers. Understanding self-image will help producers to fit the product into each consumer's image of how he or she would like to be perceived. The personality traits of the consumer can be reflected in the product, and it can also be designed to appeal to their culture. Social stratification and life-style nay also influence product development.

CASE STUDY – Researching consumer needs (pages 76/77)

1. The market has changed considerably over the last 25 years: for example, in the numbers and types of washing machines, the range of fabrics used, changes in social patterns, family sizes, occupations and leisure pursuits.
2. Market research helps them to respond to changing patterns of consumer needs by providing new and improved products to the market place.
3. If P&G had not researched their market they could have found that sales of their products declined, that they had lost market share and that their profits were affected.

TASK – page 77

Sales representatives could provide information on changing market trends and preferences as well as regular feedback on products and other first-hand views of customers.

CASE STUDY – The electricity distribution company (page 78)

1. Answers to such questions will help the company to anticipate changes in demand, and be able to respond more effectively with appropriate goods and services. They might also help the company to put together a marketing plan, identify areas in which to expand, and improve the ways in which the business is managed.
2. Other questions which might be answered include:
   - How is the market divided?
   - How does electricity usage vary?
   - When is electricity usage greatest?
   - Is it possible to discriminate between consumers?
   - How might customers respond to cash discounts?

CASE STUDY – Jus-rol Ltd (pages 82 – 84)

1. Answers will provide Jus-rol with a good idea about: purchasing patterns; the use of the product; the type of person who buys the product; their views upon quality and size; their ideas. Such information may be used to gear the product towards different groups of consumers. It may also be used to modify or improve the product or allow other strategic or tactical decisions about its future to be made.
2. The questions are all easy to understand and lack ambiguity. The questions are all closed except for questions 3 and 9.
3. Answers might vary. On the whole the questionnaire is well structured and would probably be very easy to analyse.
4. The information should be recorded in a database and then displayed using a graphics package.
5. These could then be used for sending direct mail, samples, further questionnaires, etc.

TASK – pages 86/87

Angles for the pie chart in degrees would be: 135, 36, 27, 72, and 90 respectively.

CASE STUDY – Mintel on personal savings (page 88)

1. AB are the top two socio-economic consumer groupings.
2. The Report would be useful for the providers of Tessas. It might indicate the types of Tessa taken up and the number of people taking them. It could provide ideas for selling them.
3. The results have been presented in the form of a pie chart. The format used (three-dimensional) gives it depth and makes it more interesting to look at.

CASE STUDY – Market research reports (page 88)

1. Tourists desert Mediterranean – Might be of use for travel agents, tour operators and airlines.
Sober reading – Will be of use to brewers.
Increases in home shopping – May be of use to retailers, market research agencies and providers of direct mail and warehousing facilities.
PR agencies need a PR job – This will be of use to PR and advertising agencies.
2. Reports would indicate trends, the state of markets and contain valuable information which has been extensively researched.
3. Such reports are likely to carry a high price tag to reflect the degree of labour-intensive research that has gone into their compilation.

THE MARKETING PROCESS

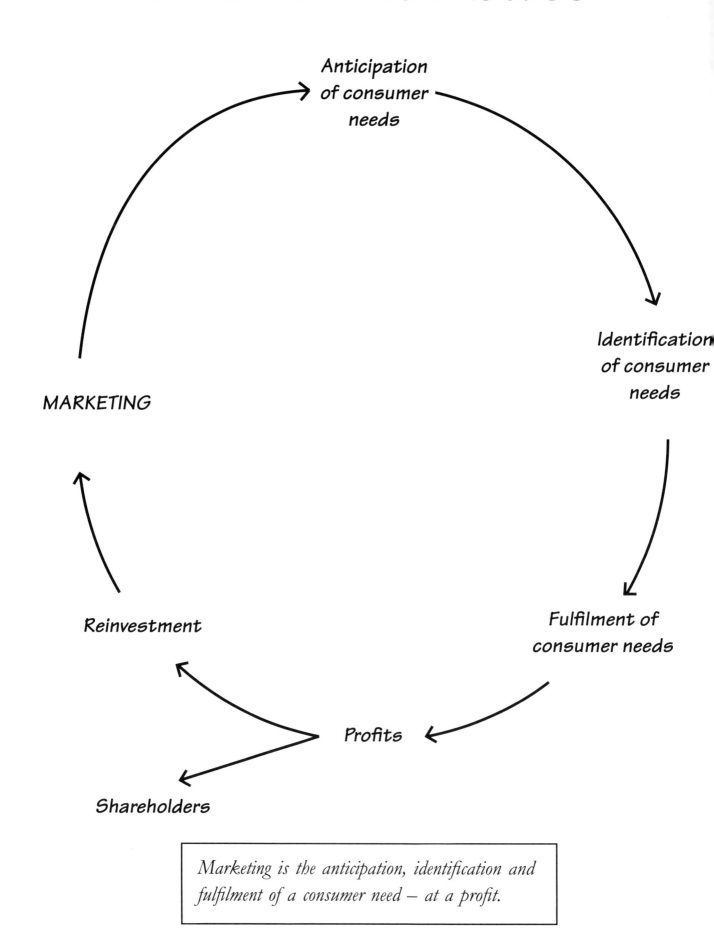

Marketing is the anticipation, identification and fulfilment of a consumer need – at a profit.

THE STEPS IN A MARKETING PLAN

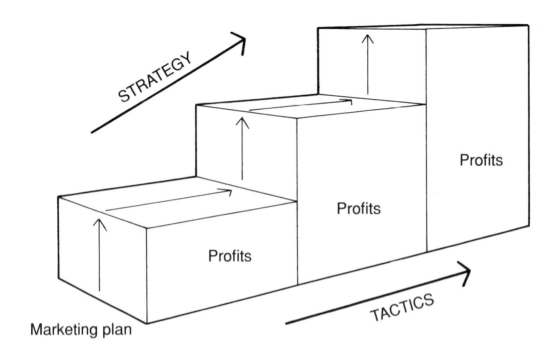

MARKETING STRATEGY is a process which develops broad objectives as well as the means for achieving them.

MARKETING TACTICS are the methods used to meet strategic goals.

'Marketing is the Generalship of business'

UNDERSTANDING CUSTOMER BEHAVIOUR

(a) *Types of customers:*

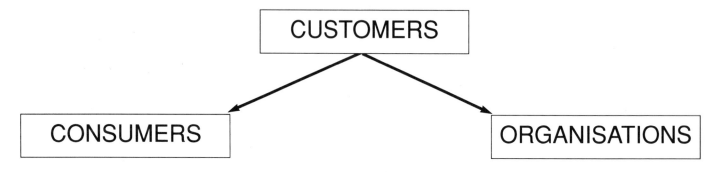

(b) *Influences upon consumers:*

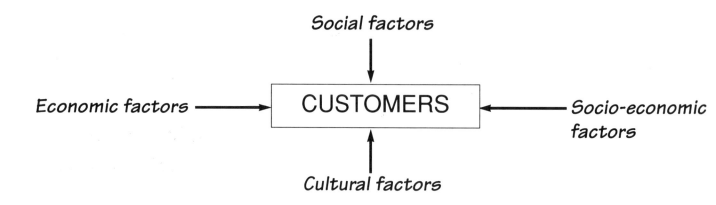

(c) *Influences upon organisations:*

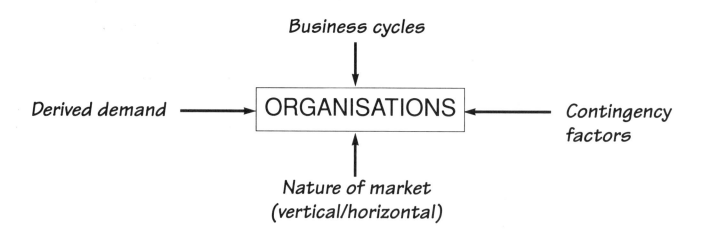

MARKET RESEARCH

MARKET RESEARCH is the systematic gathering, recording and analysis of data about problems related to the marketing of goods and services.

* Systematic – using an organised and clear method or system.

* Gathering – knowing what you are looking for, and collecting appropriate information.

* Recording – keeping clear and organised records of what you find out.

* Problems related to marketing – finding out the answers to questions that will help you to understand your customers and other details in the marketplace.

THE QUESTIONNAIRE

Questionnaire design is crucial to the survey.

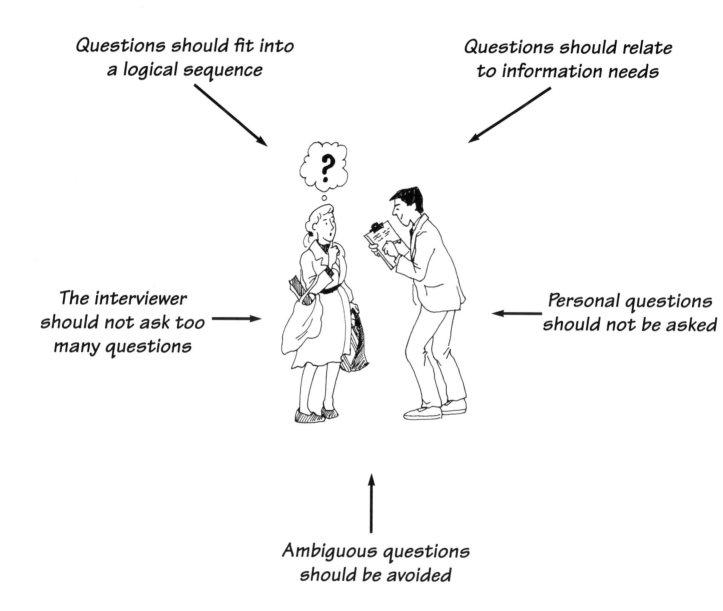

A badly designed questionnaire may lead to biased results.

Chapter 5 The Market-place

Notes for OHPs

OHP 5.1 *The Market-place*
This OHP refers to some of the key issues underlying the operation of any market and relates to pages 89 – 91 of the text. It provides a definition of a market and then shows the nature of the interactions between the buyer and the seller. It illustrates the factors influencing the power of the consumer.

OHP 5.2 *Market equilibrium*
This OHP looks at how the interaction of demand and supply forms the equilibrium price. It refers to work on the equilibrium on page 102 of the text. The diagrams are followed up with two short illustrative talks which may be used to emphasise market dynamics.

OHP 5.3 *SWOT analysis*

OHP 5.4 *Target customers*

OHP 5.5 *Media plan*
These OHPs are designed to be used to support the Group Task which runs from page 104 to page 109. the OHPs may be used to illustrate how the exercise should be undertaken and may also be used to take responses from the group during its operation.

Responses to selected Tasks and Case Studies

TASK – page 89
1. Buyers and sellers would meet regularly at the local shops, when paying a fare on a bus, when buying petrol, etc.
2. Buyers and sellers would rarely meet when buying insurance, when selling a home, booking a holiday, etc.
3. Buyers and sellers would never meet when shopping by post with mail order, if somebody makes a purchase on your behalf, with the purchase of shares, etc.

TASK – page 90
1. Accept any examples where consumers probably spend a lot of their income and where there is clearly a lot of competitive activity in the market. The influence consumers have in such circumstances should relate to the points made on page 90.
2. Consumers will have little influence in many situations, particularly where monopolies or near monopolies exist (e.g. gas, electricity).
3. The consumer clearly has power in certain circumstances and not in others. Boycotts have become a regular feature of consumer activities. Greater consumer awareness today means that consumers are increasingly likely to stand up for their rights.

TASK – page 91
1. Products for under ten customers might include bridges, ships, an office block, a television programme. Answers could include anything which is fairly unique.
2. Products which appeal to a few hundred customers might include a housing development, a number of prints from a painting, a clothing design, a type of furniture.
3. Products with a nationwide appeal may include food products, consumables, gadgets, fashion items.
4. Products with a global demand may include baby milk, cigarettes, cars, electrical products.

TASK – page 92
The purpose is for students to use their judgement to identify a price and make them think about why others may be unsuitable. They may refer in their answer to the fact that some prices are too high, unrealistic, that they do not relate to the prices of other products in the market, that people will not be able to afford the printers, etc. It would be possible to follow up the third part of the task by asking students how people would react to price rises and then use this as a basis for introducing elasticity.

TASK – page 93
1. Price has increased by 20 per cent and sales have fallen by 50 per cent. 50 divided by 20 will provide an elasticity of demand of 2.50. Demand is therefore elastic.
2. Price has increased by 20 per cent and sales have fallen by 16.66 per cent. 16.66 divided by 20 will provide an elasticity of demand of 0.83. Demand is therefore inelastic.
3. Price has decreased by 20 per cent and sales have increased by 20 per cent. Elasticity of demand will be unitary.
4. Price has been reduced by 10 per cent and the number of passengers increases by 25 per cent, giving an elasticity of 2.50. Demand is elastic.

TASK – page 94
The purpose of this series of questions is to illustrate how different strategies may influence the elasticity of a product over time. For example, a product which is unique today will be inelastic and, as other similar products enter the market place, the product will become more elastic. Conversely, a product which exists in an elastic market may, through a series of modifications, product improvements, promotions and other developments, be made more unique, and elasticity could become more inelastic.

TASK – pages 97/98
1. The demand curve for fiction books will shift to the left.
2. The demand curve for designer clothes for children will shift to the right.
3. The demand curve for films will probably remain about the same.
4. The demand curve for newspapers will shift to the left.
5. The demand curve for ice-cream cornets will shift to the right.
6. The demand curve for fireworks will probably remain about the same.

CASE STUDY – The changing demand for white bread (page 98)
1. Answers might include white, wholemeal, brown bread, wheatgerm and ethnic bread.
2. White bread sales fell during the 1980s but started to rise again in recent years. Factors may have included the rising price of substitutes, falling incomes and changes in tastes. Wholemeal bread sales increased during the 1980s. However, with white bread recently developing a larger market share this could be at the expense of wholemeal. Factors would be similar to the above.
3. The answer should mention market research and contain a series of relevant questions.
4. The figures seem to indicate price as the predominant factor and show that white bread seems to be doing well.

Section 2 – The Client

TASK – page 99

1. The demand curve will shift to the right.
2. The demand curve will shift to the right.
3. The demand curve will shift to the left.
4. The demand curve will shift to the left.
5. Either no increase or a shift to the left.
6. The demand curve will shift to the left.
7. This may prompt a discussion! The demand curve would shift to the left if fish shops buy their supplies of newspapers.

TASK – page 100

1.
   a. 25 million
   b. 22½ million
   c. 20 million
   d. 17 million
   e. 15 million
   f. 13½ million
   g. 12½ million
   h. 8 million

2. The supply curve slopes downwards from the top right to the bottom left. Producers will be willing to supply more at higher prices. Its shape may be determined by time, capacity, availability and costs.

TASK – page 102

a. Shift the supply curve to the right.
b. Supply will remain the same (perfectly inelastic).
c. Shift the supply curve to the right.
d. Shift the supply curve to the left.
e. Shift the supply curve of large-engined cars to the left.

THE MARKET-PLACE

A market exists when buyers and sellers come into contact.

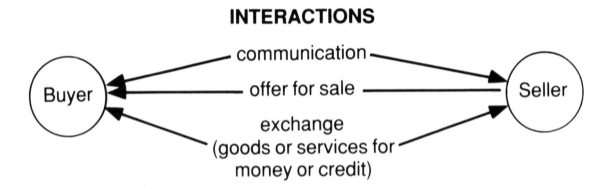

The power of the consumer depends upon:

* *their income*
* *the extent of their buying power*
* *the nature of the competition*
* *the proportion they purchase*
* *whether they are organised into buying groups*
* *whether they are informed*
* *whether they are protected*

MARKET EQUILIBRIUM

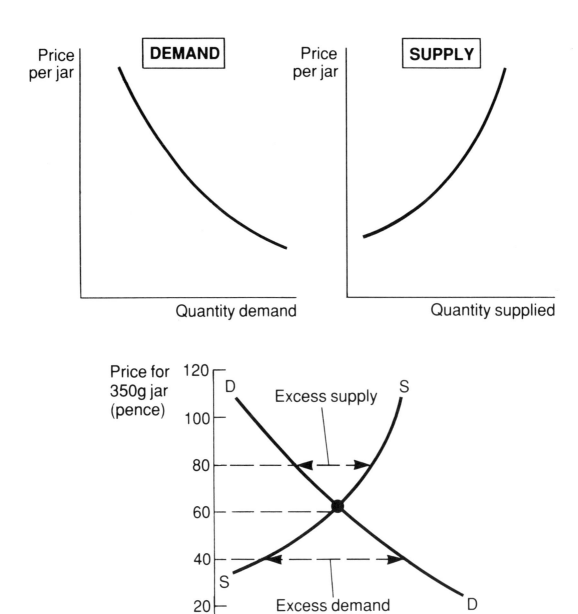

Producers and consumers respond to price signals and in this way their wishes and plans are coordinated by the price mechanism.

Task 1 – What might happen to the market for tobacco products if a blight affects the South American crop?

Task 2 – What would happen to the market for heavy boots if it became fashionable to wear them?

SWOT ANALYSIS

PRODUCT_____

STRENGTHS	WEAKNESSES
OPPORTUNITIES	THREATS

OHP 5.4

TARGET CUSTOMERS

PRODUCT _____

STATUS	AGE	INCOME H – HIGH L – LOW	TARGET AUDIENCE	SUITABLE MEDIA
MALE (MARRIED) NO CHILDREN	18 – 24	H		
		L		
	25 – 45	H		
		L		
	OVER 45	H		
		L		
FEMALE (MARRIED) NO CHILDREN	18 – 24	H		
		L		
	25 – 45	H		
		L		
	OVER 45	H		
		L		
MALE (MARRIED) + CHILDREN	18 – 24	H		
		L		
	25 – 45	H		
		L		
	OVER 45	H		
		L		
FEMALE (MARRIED) + CHILDREN	18 – 24	H		
		L		
	25 – 45	H		
		L		
	OVER 45	H		
		L		
MALE (SINGLE)	18 – 24	H		
		L		
	25 – 45	H		
		L		
	OVER 45	H		
		L		
FEMALE (SINGLE)	18 – 24	H		
		L		
	25 – 45	H		
		L		
	OVER 45	H		
		L		

OHP 5.5

MEDIA PLAN

PRODUCT _____

MEDIA		£ COST	JAN	FEB	MAR	APR	MAY	JUN	JUL	AUG	SEP	OCT	NOV	DEC	SUB-TOTAL COSTS	COMMENTS
TELEVISION (CENTRAL AREA)	30 SECOND TV COMMERCIAL OCT, NOV, DEC, MAR, APR, MAY — OFF PEAK	600														
	30 SECOND TV COMMERCIAL OCT, NOV, DEC, MAR, APR, MAY — ON PEAK	4,000														
	30 SECOND TV COMMERCIAL JAN, FEB, JUN, JUL, AUG, SEP — OFF PEAK	400														
	30 SECOND TV COMMERCIAL JAN, FEB, JUN, JUL, AUG, SEP — ON PEAK	3,000														
LOCAL RADIO	30 SECOND SPOT	100														
NATIONAL PRESS	ONE INSERTION PER NEWSPAPER	5,000														
LOCAL PRESS	ONE INSERTION PER NEWSPAPER	500														
FREE TRADE PRESS	ONE INSERTION PER NEWSPAPER	200														
ELECTRICITY ACCOUNT INSERTS	ONE FOR EACH DOMESTIC CUSTOMER PER QUARTER	30,000														
DIRECT MAILING	1000 PACKAGES DELIVERED BY THE POST OFFICE (SELECTED ADDRESSES)	450														
	1000 PACKAGES HAND-DELIVERED (SELECTED AREAS)	300														
TELEPHONE SALES	PER HUNDRED CALLS	10														
EXHIBITIONS	SMALL	250														
	MEDIUM	1,500														
	LARGE	4,000														
LEAFLETS	PER THOUSAND	250														
SHOP DISPLAYS	76 SHOPS	10,000														

Section 2 – The Client

Chapter 6 Marketing Products and Services

Notes for OHPs

OHP 6.1 *Market segmentation*
This OHP refers to the market segmentation process outlined on pages 112 and 113 of the text. As well as defining the process of segmentation, it endeavours to highlight the differences between an organisation which tries to serve a range of needs with a single product and an organisation which identifies the needs of specific groups of customers and targets its products towards them. An organisation which uses the blunderbuss approach is less marketing orientated because it does not serve the requirements of customers as well as the organisation which segments its market. It may be possible to follow up the OHP by asking students to identify organisations which offer a single mix to a whole market and compare them with organisations clearly segmenting their markets.

OHP 6.2 *The marketing mix*
This OHP defines the marketing mix, illustrates its ingredients and indicates that each mix can be used to suit the precise requirements of each market or segment. It refers to page 114 of the text.

OHP 6.3 *The product*
This OHP highlights the various aspects of the product part of the marketing mix which appears on pages 115 and 116 of the text. It outlines the tangible benefits, intangible features, generic dimensions, sensual dimensions and extended dimensions.

OHP 6.4 *Using the marketing mix*
The marketing mix is an important strategic and tactical device. Each mix represents a unique blend designed to achieve an organisation's objectives. In this OHP the differences between undifferentiated, differentiated and concentrated techniques are highlighted. Such techniques enable an organisation to undertake a positioning strategy which creates a differential advantage over rivals. See page 130 of the text.

OHP 6.5 *The product life-cycle*
This OHP refers to pages 131 and 132 of the text. it can be used to highlight the various stages of the life-cycle, injections into the life-cycle and the product portfolio.

Responses to selected Tasks and Case Studies

CASE STUDY – Computers in schools (page 111)

1. Students would probably be able to answer parts of this question from their own first-hand experiences. Answers might include:
   a Acorn machines are easy to use, flexible and designed for the educational market.
   b The biggest reason for their success must be the range of software available and their general acceptability for the educational market.
   c Few other competitors have designed a machine which is as closely dedicated to the needs and requirements of the educational market.
   d The large market size enables Acorn to specialise, provides them with economies of scale, enables them to develop long production runs with a larger margin, allows them strategic flexibility.
   e The direct competition would be RM. Indirect competition would be PCs.
2. The survey would have highlighted market share, size of market and nearest competitors. It enables Acorn to know who their competitors are and then develop strategies which are more suited to educational needs than those of their nearest rivals.
3. If computers are about a thousand pounds each, the total value of the market will be more than £100 million.

CASE STUDY – Credit card services (page 113)

1. a National Westminster Bank can tailor credit cards to certain customers. It can give customers a choice. Over a long period of time it might bring in more revenue.
   b Customers can appreciate a range of different services which are linked to their particular style of life. Different cards can provide different services.
2. A blunderbuss strategy provides a single marketing mix for the whole market, whereas segmenting a market will target a marketing strategy at a particular group of customers.
3. Segmentation may take place according to: social factors; cultural factors; socio-economic factors; personality; life-style.
4. An organisation must monitor its range strategy to cater for changing circumstances and different customer needs. Not doing so would eventually lead of loss of market share.

CASE STUDY – New product development in Japan (pages 117/118)

1. European companies find it difficult to compete in Japan because they see their products matched and then left behind, beaten by rapid innovation.
2. Rushing out products too quickly means that products are not sufficiently tested.
3. a Product covering is the process of rushing out instant imitations.
   b Product churning takes product covering further and involves the constant churning out of new products until they find one which is successful.
   c Parallel development involves developing a new generation of products to supersede the original along with the original.
4. The Japanese save time and capital expenditure by using off-the-shelf components.
5. a Good marketing practices would include: quality products in volume at low prices; rapid innovation; developing further generations of products along with the original; investment in education; free flow of information.
   b Poor marketing practices may include: copying other ideas; rushing out imitations many of which are not tested; wasting of product ideas.
6. Japanese consumers have a wide choice of low-price volume products that are constantly changing.

TASK – page 122

BT adjusts its pricing three times a day. Other forms of price discrimination might include car prices overseas, the different types of services offered by British Rail, off-peak electricity charges, etc.

CASE STUDY – Car wars (pages 123/124)

1. Car sales plunged in 1991 mainly because of the recession. As sales fell manufacturers engaged in a price war.
2. Pricing techniques included:
   - demand-orientated – prices fell as demand fell
   - competition-orientated – producers followed the actions of each other
   - destroyer pricing – to undermine the actions of rivals
   - promotional pricing – to inject new life into the market.
3. Those who benefit might include: both consumers and organisations who make vehicle purchases; the economy, as lower prices for vehicles mean lower inflation; individuals and households affected by the trend towards lower prices.
4. The answers to this question are endless, but might include line extensions, product modification, better advertising, sales promotions and public relations.
5. People will in general hold on to their cars longer. The recession and company liquidations may increase the number of second-hand cars coming on-stream. Consumers may now opt to buy second-hand cars as opposed to new cars.

CASE STUDY – Developing a fast answer to fashion fads (pages 125/126)

1. Quick Responses (QR) equates demand more closely with supply by shortening the lead time on new products.
2. QR involves getting the right product to the right place in the quickest possible time. Having an effective distribution system is essential if it is to work.
3. Customers, retailers, manufacturers and shareholders all benefit from QR.
4. Retail technology such as EPOS can quickly identify best selling lines from which trends can be identified.
5. Answers might include books, toys, CDs, videos and any other market where the products constantly change.
6. This question is wide open to imaginative solutions and may be best worked at in group discussion. Answers might include: retail technology; relationships with suppliers; the production of their own goods; retail audits.

CASE STUDY – Ski uses rock 'n' roll for cerebral palsy (pages 129/130)

1. Some organisations consider it a responsibility. It makes the organisation look favourable and is good PR.
2. Comments may vary.
3. In the short term it may stimulate sales, while in the long term it will help to build and develop the image of the brand.

CASE STUDY – Bringing Kettle Chips to Britain (pages 132/133)

1. A premium priced product is a product priced highly because of quality, image, name, positioning strategy, etc.
2. Nearly all of the emphasis in the mix is on a high price, quality product and distribution deals with no promotion. If no such deals took place it would undoubtedly mean that Kettle Chips would not be able to afford the big advertising spend of its rivals. Everything depends on continued demands for the product and arrangement of distribution deals.
3. Ideas may vary.
4. Kettle Chips will probably remain successful as long as its products remain popular and as long as it can continue to arrange distribution deals. In order to keep the brand popular the company will have to update the product continually to cater for changing tastes and to be viewed as exciting. New types of Kettle Chips will, therefore, be essential.

Supporting Notes for Part B – The Client

Further areas to explore

This section is essentially concerned with marketing and, as marketing is about planning, it will tie in very closely with the work in Chapter 18, which builds and develops the planning process further: for example, in terms of personal action planning, strategic audit, organisational planning and change.

With the development of the EC Single Market, one useful area to explore is the marketing of products overseas. Students should be made aware of why we need to sell our products abroad and of the benefits of one large single market. They should be encouraged to think about the differences between marketing in a domestic market and in an overseas market and how such a process should take place.

Another area to look at is the wider responsibilities which organisations should undertake when they decide to market a range of products and services. For example, what responsibilities does a tobacco manufacturer have to its customers? Within this context, it would be useful to develop the area further by looking at consumerism, consumer protection, environmentalism, and marketing ethics. As consumer power increases and develops over the next few years, these areas are likely to assume increasing importance for more and more organisations.

Both of the above areas can be looked at in our book *Marketing – Everybody's Business*, which is published by Heinemann Educational.

Assignment ideas and suggestions

'Marketing' should be viewed as a practical area in which students are encouraged to engage in a series of mini-activities and assignments. Such activities may relate to their own work-based experiences or to wider situations. The situations do not have to be complex. Of all the areas in which assignments are written, this is probably one of the easiest in which to develop both real and fictitious tasks. It is also a very useful area from which to develop an assignment that integrates other parts of the core realistically. Another important point to make is that, having covered this unit, it is not one to be forgotten, but one which should be built upon and reinforced within other units later in the course.

Working in small groups, students can be asked to choose a product or service. They could then use both desk and field research to find out more about both the market in which the product exists as well as how consumers feel about it. Feedback and presentation should involve use of IT facilities. Using such research they may then identify:

- the market segments in which their product or service is designed to appeal
- its current phase in its life-cycle
- the elements of its marketing mix.

Students may then be encouraged to think more widely about the product's future. To do this they should conduct a SWOT analysis, assess further product possibilities (such as modifications and line-extensions), consider the other ingredients of the mix and how they could be matched in to any changes, and then present their results in the form of a plan. Using appropriate presentation techniques, the plan could be presented to the rest of the group.

Though the above is very broad, this sort of approach is simple, straightforward and easy to develop further.

MARKET SEGMENTATION

- An organisation cannot serve its customers well if it groups all of their needs and wants together.

- Instead of trying to serve all customers equally, it may focus its efforts upon different parts of the total market-place.

- Within the total market-place it is possible to group customers with similar characteristics into market segments.

Supplying a single product to the whole market to satisfy everybody's different needs is like using a blunderbuss, firing shots to pepper the whole market-place.

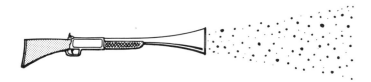

Market segmentation enables an organisation to divide customers into small market segments consisting of buyers with similar needs or characteristics. Customers can be targeted more efficiently.

THE MARKETING MIX

The marketing mix comprises a series of variables which an organisation can combine in order to achieve its objectives.

The concept is usually analysed on the basis of the four P's. To meet customer needs an organisation must develop <u>products</u> to satisfy them, charge the right <u>price</u>, get the goods to the right <u>place</u> and make the existence of the product known through its <u>promotion</u>.

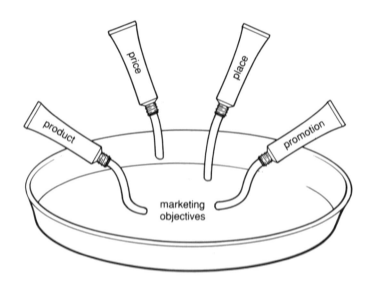

Each mix can be used to suit the precise requirements of each market or segment.

THE PRODUCT

Tangible benefits:	• shape • design • colour • packaging • size • appearance
Intangible features:	• after-sales service • availability of spare parts • customer care policy • guarantees
Generic dimensions:	the key benefits of an item which involve what the product does (e.g. shoe polish cleans shoes)
Sensual dimensions:	provide sensual benefits such as design, colour, taste and smell
Extended dimensions:	include additional benefits such as servicing agreements, credit facilities, guarantees etc.

USING THE MARKETING MIX

With <u>undifferentiated</u> marketing, a single marketing mix is offered to the total market-place.

<u>Differentiated</u> marketing is the strategy of attacking the market-place by tailoring separate product and marketing strategies to different sectors of the market.

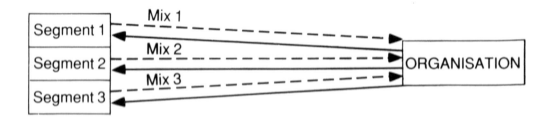

<u>Concentrated</u> marketing involves choosing to compete in one segment developing the most effective mix for this sub-market.

Organisations will try to create a <u>differential</u> advantage over their rivals. A <u>positioning</u> strategy will involve selecting a market segment and creating a differential advantage over rivals in that area.

OHP 6.5

THE PRODUCT LIFE-CYCLE

Stages in the product life-cycle:

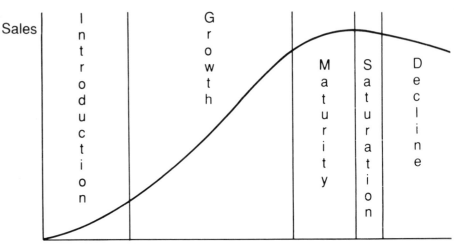

Periodic injections into the product life-cycle:

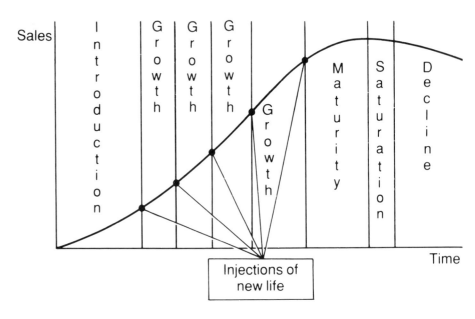

The product portfolio:

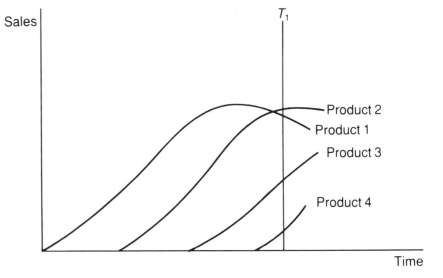

SECTION 2

Part C – The Administration

One of the purposes of the BTEC National course in Business and Finance is to provide students with a broad understanding of administrative activities, procedures and systems. We felt that it was important to identify the level of administrative activities at which most students will engage in their careers. The assumption which we have drawn was extracted from the first draft specification pack, where it pointed out that students would be involved in a complex series of administrative tasks, many of which will involve supervising others. We also felt that this might involve taking responsibility for the effective operation of a team.

Administering an activity involves a need to organise, control and make decisions. An administrator generally has to take responsibility not only for his or her actions, but also for the activities of others. Under the administrative theme we have identified three central areas.

Chapter 7 – Communication analyses the different levels of administration as well as their nature and purpose. It looks at communication within the context of administration. Basic communication skills are studied and supported by a number of practical tasks and then both internal and external communication are outlined in detail.

Chapter 8 – Using Information Technology in Organisations examines the different ways in which IT supports the administrative process. All organisations process a great deal of information and, in the modern world, information technology lies at the heart of effective data management. This chapter explores many of the features of modern technology, including the uses of packages and other recent developments. Many of the activities within this chapter are designed to encourage students to think about their own IT capabilities and what they need to do to improve their existing skills.

Chapter 9 – People in their Working Environment is concerned with how people work together in their workplace. The chapter looks at ways of achieving co-operation and improving contributions from the workforce, including teamwork, meetings and the use of quality circles and training. In this chapter we look closely at the roles of these areas and assess how each contributes to improving the quality of life in the working environment.

Chapter 7 Communication

Notes for OHPs

OHP 7.1 *The levels of administrative activity*
This OHP refers to the short section at the beginning of Chapter 7 on pages 134 and 135. The section is designed to introduce the administrative function and this OHP relates four broad areas of administrative activities to the levels of management or administration.

OHP 7.2 *The communication process*
The communication process involves the sending of a message from a sender to a receiver. This OHP refers to pages 137 and 138 of the text. It can be used to highlight the various stages of the communication process and can then be used to discuss the different forms of noise which interfere with the smooth flow of information.

OHP 7.3 *Basic communication skills*
This OHP can be used to introduce and then highlight the four basic communication skills from pages 138 to 140 of the text. The four traditional skills are listening, speaking, writing and reading. The latter two have been transformed by the use of IT. In the text we say that 'IT skills are the penmanship of the future'. It might be worth following up the upper half of this OHP by asking students why we say this. The lower half of the OHP refers to the use of body language and can be used – perhaps with practical examples – to emphasise the importance of physical gestures and facial expressions.

OHP 7.4 *Internal and external communications*
This OHP visually details the different forms of internal and external communication which appear from pages 141 to 152 of the text. The OHP can be used to introduce each form of communication so that they can be briefly identified before moving ahead to assess them in more detail.

OHP 7.5 *Parts of a business letter*
This OHP refers to pages 148 and 149 of the text. It can be used to highlight the various parts of a business letter.

Responses to selected Tasks and Case Studies

CASE STUDY – Transforming EMI (page 135)

1 This first task is designed so that students can think about – or perhaps discuss in groups – the role and importance of people in administration. Answers will vary widely but should provide important feedback, from which it may be possible to discuss the contributions individuals provide to an organisation and how their efforts may influence others.
2 This task enables you to refer to the different levels of administrative activity and emphasise that central to each of these stages is the communication process. It may be possible to follow this up by discussing what might happen in an organisation where communication links were bad.

TASK – page 136

Though you will probably receive a variety of responses, the truth is that just about all positions of employment involve some semblance of managerial skills.

CASE STUDY – A man of influence (page 140)

1 Key skills used by Jean Peyrelevade include: the ability to put forward a strong case; being able to identify key issues; being direct; honesty; a willingness to tackle rather than evade issues; being prepared to explain his position. Such an approach requires well-developed speaking skills.
2 Students should point out that anyone who influences others should have good communication skills.
3 A good speaker can make a talk interesting. Listening to such a speaker may motivate, educate, encourage, inform, support etc. Students may relate their answers to their own experiences. Ask them who they think is a good speaker and why.

CASE STUDY – Darlo Holdings (page 143)

1. Advantages may include: better communications; may be used to motivate staff; staff can generate ideas and provide feedback; many staff want to be listened to; employees may prefer to work as part of a team.

    Disadvantages may include: some may view this as a waste of time; many may prefer the old system; could put employees under pressure to contribute; change might be resisted.
2. Speaking skills will vary. Encouraging all employees to regularly contribute to meetings may require training which builds their confidence and shows them how to become an effective speaker.

TASK – page 144

The memo should be simple and straightforward in order to be effective.

CASE STUDY – St Michael News (pages 145/146)

1. Management place emphasis upon partnership with employees because such a partnership will motivate, improve commitment, provide feedback, improve industrial relations, etc.
2. Such a partnership cannot exist without a good communication system. If employees are to be kept informed, there must be an effective system which allows this to happen.
3. Answers might include: notices; distribution of minutes and agendas; availability of reports; memos; use of phone; meetings; face-to-face exchanges.

TASK – page 147

Rules may include a range of suggestions, which could be similar to many of the points made in Figure 7.8 on page 142.

TASK – page 148

Advantages of using written communications outside the organisation may include: the communication may be re-read; it may be used to enhance image or reputation; it may be persuasive; it can relay technical details.

    Disadvantages of using written communications outside the organisation may include: the communication may be badly written or contain mistakes; many people ignore written communications, particularly if they are complex; the communication may soon become outdated and need revising.

TASK – page 149

Each letter should be carefully checked, perhaps by other members of the group, so that feedback can be provided.

CASE STUDY – Interruptions to electricity supplies (page 150)

1. At the time there were many disgruntled consumers who felt that, despite the weather conditions, supplies should not have been interrupted for as long as they were. It was essential for the MD of Northern Electric to placate consumers with an explanation about what had happened and a description of how they had tackled the problem.
2. Writing such a letter would have been difficult. The MD realised the need to respond to consumers but wished neither to offend consumers nor admit to any negligence.
3. Many students may seem happy with the communication. Others may comment upon how it has been written.

CASE STUDY – Videoconferencing coming of age in the Gulf war (page 151)

1. Videoconferencing may provide savings on travel costs, accommodation, catering expenses; savings in time will help to maximise the efficient use of manpower; savings on conference costs, entertainment, etc.
2. Other benefits may include: better links with other parts of an organisation, companies, customers etc.; speed; improvements in quality of decision making.
3. Videoconferencing may help organisations to respond more readily to the market, make decisions more quickly, work together more cohesively, minimise influence of diseconomies, etc.

CASE STUDY – British Nuclear Fuels PLC (pages 151/152)

1. By the very nature of its activities BNFL is of interest to the public. To counter hostile feelings and provide interested parties with a positive picture of its work, it has to invest heavily in public relations. Without such a process BNFL might see many of its activities hampered by a disapproving public.
2. Sellafield Visitors Centre – visual and written; site tours – visual; travelling exhibition – visual and written; computer program – visual and written; talks service – verbal, visual and probably written; publications – written and visual; films – visual and verbal.

OHP 7.1

THE LEVELS OF ADMINISTRATIVE ACTIVITY

	Level of management or administration		
	Senior	Middle	Lower
Planning	▓▓▓▓	▓▓	▓
Organising	▓	▓▓▓▓	▓▓
Controlling	▓▓	▓▓▓▓	▓▓
Doing	▓	▓	▓▓▓▓

- PLANNING – *deciding what provisions need to be made in the future*
- ORGANISING – *making sure that all resources are available at the right moment.*
- CONTROLLING – *making sure that things happen as they were planned.*
- DOING – *becoming actively involved in the task at hand.*

THE COMMUNICATION PROCESS

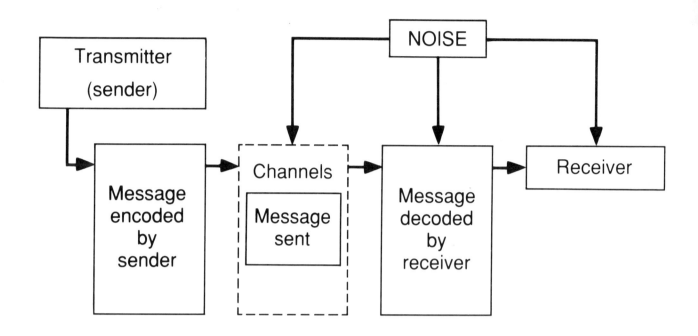

The *transmitter* sends messages to receivers.

Encoding puts information in a form receivers can understand.

Channels may include letter, report, fax etc.

Decoding involves the interpretation of messages.

Noise involves any barriers which interfere with the flow of information.

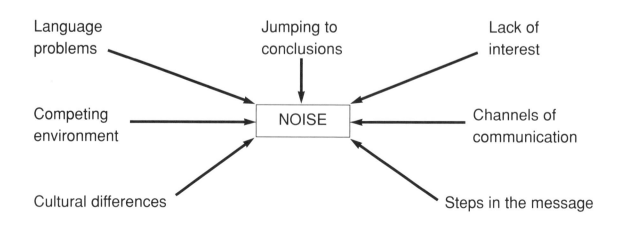

BASIC COMMUNICATION SKILLS

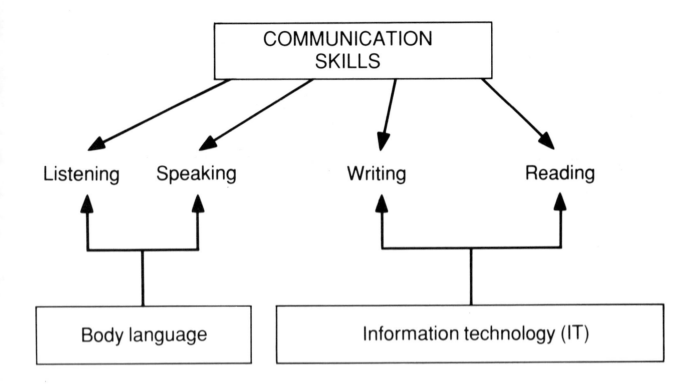

Communication skills cover listening, speaking, reading, writing and the use of information technology (IT).

BODY LANGUAGE

PHYSICAL GESTURES

FACIAL EXPRESSIONS

INTERNAL AND EXTERNAL COMMUNICATIONS

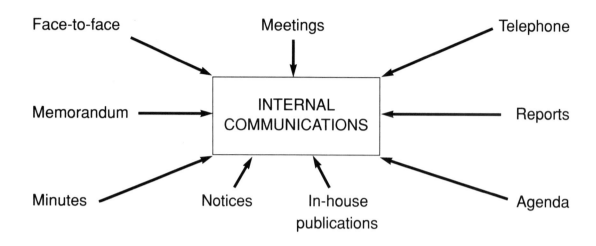

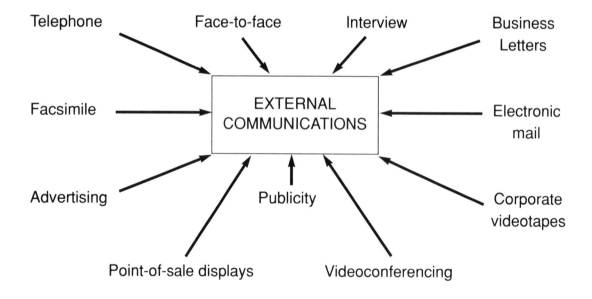

PARTS OF A BUSINESS LETTER

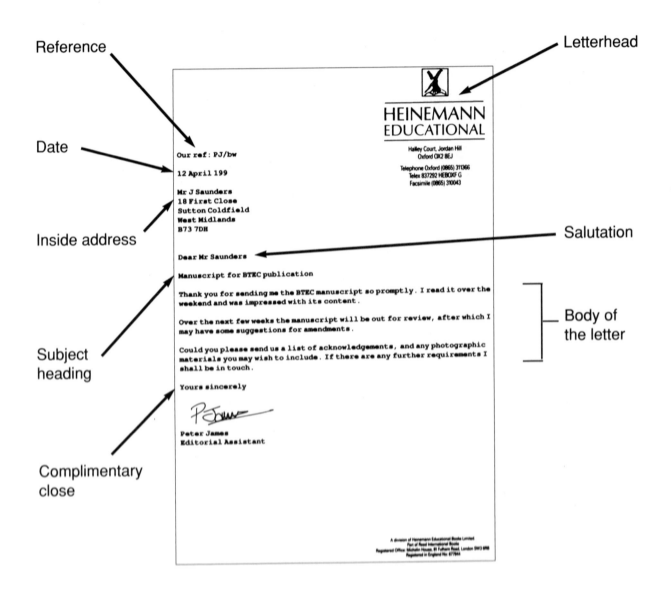

Section 2 – The Administration

Chapter 8 Using Information Technology in Organisations

Notes for OHPs

OHP 8.1 *IT applications in your college*
This OHP refers to the task which appears on page 153 of the text. The chart which illustrates some IT applications in college is highlighted. Underneath there is a space for the other applications identified by students. These might include: DTP for internal publications; electronic display board; electronic mail; information systems; CD ROMs etc.

OHP 8.2 *Information technology skills*
IT skills are identified on pages 154 and 155 of the book. The two diagrams on this OHP can be used to emphasise the users of IT in the workplace and some of the general IT skills.

OHP 8.3 *Desktop publishing*
This OHP refers to the work on desktop publishing which appears on page 159 of the text. It shows a layout produced by DTP. Underneath this is the task from the same page. You might wish to use this to illustrate what you require on the title page and to help you to advise students about its completion.

OHP 8.4 *The spreadsheet*
This spreadsheet is intended to accompany the tasks on pages 161 and 162. You might wish to fill in parts of the chart to help students with the figures, or use it to go through the spreadsheet when near completion or when dealing with the 'what if?' situations. Monthly sales income is expected to be: petrol £120 000, lubricants £1300, confectionery £4000, fastfood £700, groceries £900, accessories £1200, newspapers/magazines £1000, toys/greetings cards £300, books/tapes £400 and cigarettes/tobacco £6500. Total monthly income will be £136 300. Monthly outgoings are expected to be: staff wages £3000, insurance £125, heat/light power £375, security charges £100, rent/rates £350, maintenance/repairs £175, office supplies £450, depreciation £300, petrol £90 000, lubricants £1000, stock for shop £12 500. Total monthly outgoings will be £108 375. Profit per month would therefore be £27 925 and for the year £335 100.
  a If petrol sales were twice the original, stocks would also have to be twice the original. Monthly petrol sales would then be £240 000 and monthly petrol purchases would be £180 000. As a result monthly income would rise to £256 300 and monthly outgoings would rise to £198 375. Profit for the month would now be £57 925 and for the year it would be £695 100.
  b From the original situation, if wages increase by 10 per cent in June, profit will go down by £300 per month and, assuming that the increase includes June, over the seven months it will reduce profits by £2100.
  c If rent and rates go up by 20 per cent from 1 March, profits will go down by £70 per month and over the ten months it will go down by £700.
  d If the cost of petrol and lubricants rises by 10 per cent in November with no corresponding increase in prices, profits will fall by £9100 per month and by £18 200 in total.

OHP 8.5 *IT skills checklist*
This OHP refers to the chart on page 169 and can be used to help students to complete the checklist.

Responses to selected Tasks and Case Studies

TASK – page 155

In response to this task almost any business process will suffice. Wherever possible try to emphasise how this business process is aided by IT.

TASK – page 156

The task asks 'to what extent' and answers should attempt to tackle this issue. Answers could refer to any form of IT facility. Better responses might refer to management information systems. Emphasis in students' answers might be upon the 'transformation business approach' with greater sharing of information and team working.

a The advantages of working in traditional functional organisations might include: clear established hierarchy; rules and procedures; senior managers take responsibility for decisions.
   The disadvantages might include: limited freedom for employees to make decisions; slow response to customer needs; lacks challenge.
b The advantages of working in process-based organisations might include: cost reduction with simplified work flow; improved responsiveness to customer needs; improved job satisfaction; challenging environment.
   The disadvantages might include: some staff not wishing to take responsibility for taking decisions; team working may lead to conflict; may be too flexible; can become confused and complex.

TASK – page 158

1 a The students' own records will need to be recorded and sorted. They may require some calculation, will have to be stored and will later need to be retrieved. It might be necessary to reproduce them.
  b The bank or building society statement will probably involve all processes.
2 Budgeting may involve recording, checking, classifying, sorting and some calculating.

TASK – page 160

The database might contain details such as name, age, sex, courses, employer, address. Information such as exam results, health details and references should be excluded.

TASK – page 163

Database information may help:
a the police – with records of past crimes, criminals, complaints.
b hospitals – records of patients, illnesses, staff.
c oil companies – records of employees, stocks, customers.

TASK – page 164

The three situations would probably refer to any form of scientific, technical or engineering-based application.

Using Information Technology in Organisations

CASE STUDY – The arrival of book computers (page 165)

1 Book computers are simple to use, have targeted use, are easy to use and provide privacy.
2 At the moment their use is limited but their potential is being further explored.
3 They may be used for training, as a source of data, to find cross-referenced information, for reference sources and for research.

CASE STUDY – IT at use in a service station (page 168)

Students should work in groups on this activity. Service stations to be included should be carefully selected. The case might involve sending a questionnaire to those chosen. The final reports should be presented to the rest of the group for discussion and further analysis.

OHP 8.1

IT APPLICATIONS IN YOUR COLLEGE

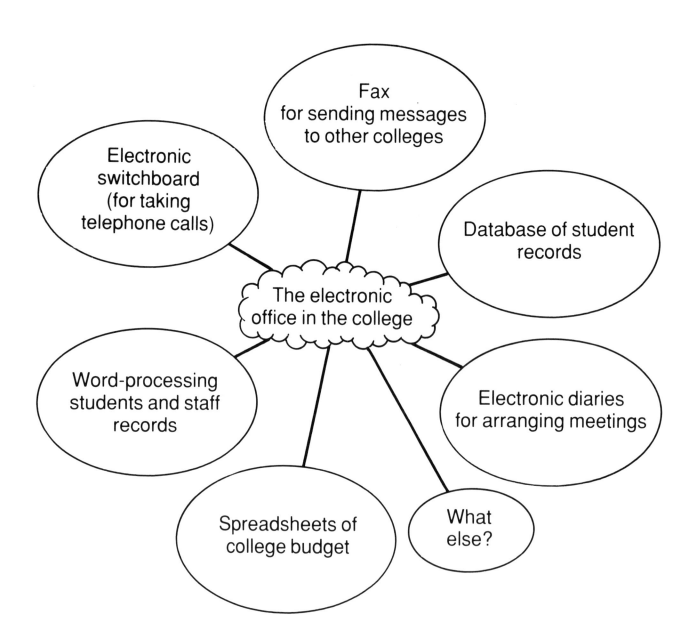

OTHERS

INFORMATION TECHNOLOGY SKILLS

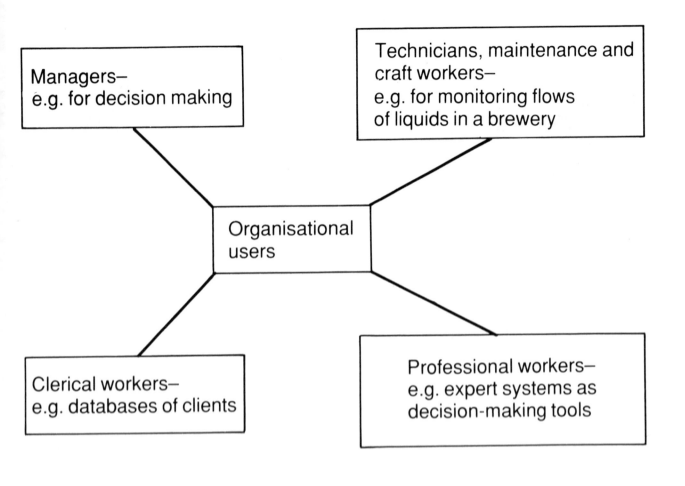

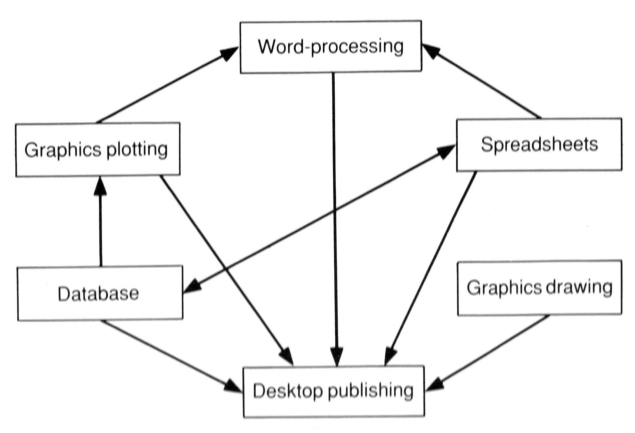

OHP 8.3

DESKTOP PUBLISHING

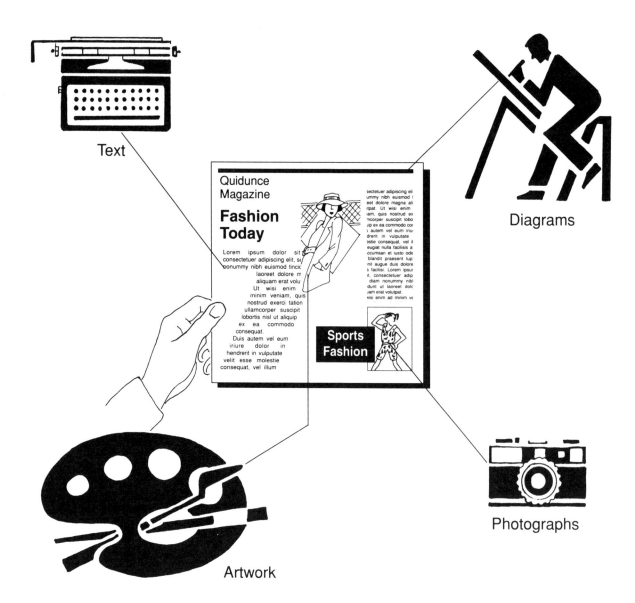

TASK

Use a desktop publishing system to produce a cover sheet that can be adapted for each of your Business Studies assignments. The cover should be designed so that you can quickly amend it to word-process the new title of each assignment.

OHP 8.4

THE SPREADSHEET

INCOME	JAN	FEB	MAR	APR	ETC.
Petrol					
Lubricants					
Confectionery					
Fast food					
Groceries					
Accessories					
Newspapers/magazines					
Toys/greetings cards					
Books/tapes					
Cigarettes/tobacco					
TOTAL INCOME					
OUTGOINGS					
Staff wages					
Insurance					
Heat/light/power					
Security charges					
Rent/rates					
Maintenance/repairs					
Office supplies					
Depreciation					
Petrol					
Lubricants					
Stock for shop					
TOTAL OUTGOINGS					

OHP 8.5

IT SKILLS CHECKLIST

IT SKILLS CHECKLIST

Indicate by a tick in the appropriate boxes what, in your opinion, is your level of **experience** with respect the skills mentioned:

1. *I am experienced at this.*
2. *I have some experience of this.*
3. *I have no experience of this.*

Indicate by a tick in the appropriate boxes what you feel to be your **success** with the skills mentioned:

1. *I was successful at this.*
2. *I was reasonably successful at this.*
3. *I was rarely successful at this.*

	Experience 1 2 3	Success 1 2 3
Using a microcomputer in any way		
Using a simple word-processing package		
Using a more complex word-processing package		
Using a drawing/painting package		
Using a desktop publishing program		
Using a multimedia program (sound/animation/graphics)		
Using a data-retrieval system		
Using a spreadsheet		
Using a printer		
Using a colour printer		
Using a plotter		
Other experiences (specify)		

Chapter 9   People in their Working Environment

Notes for OHPs

OHP 9.1   *The demographic time-bomb*
This OHP refers to the forecast changes in the employment market known as the demographic time-bomb, which appears on page 171 of the text. The OHP highlights the probable effects of the demographic time-bomb and suggests some solutions. The solutions may by used to form the basis for discussion. For example, students could be asked how easy it would be to implement each of the solutions.

OHP 9.2   *Teamwork*
This OHP defines a team and refers to the task, process and action schedule (see page 173). It then shows the diagram illustrating members working together as a team as well as the diagram illustrating how members benefit from teamwork, both of which appear on page 175.

OHP 9.3   *Group dynamics*
This OHP highlights elements of the work which appears on pages 176–178 of the text. It emphasises the importance of relating corporate objectives to group objectives, lists the advantages and disadvantages of groups, and then allows the user to show the illustration which outlines the factors affecting group dynamics.

OHP 9.4   *Leadership style*
This OHP refers to leadership and its effect upon group dynamics by highlighting autocratic leadership styles and democratic leadership styles with the two illustrations which appear on page 178.

OHP 9.5   *Meetings*
The purpose of this OHP is to provide visual support for the teaching of meetings which appears on page 179 and runs through to page 183. The OHP refers to the purposes of meetings, states what a notice of meeting and agenda are, and then briefly refers to the roles of the chairperson and the secretary.

Responses to selected Tasks and Case Studies

CASE STUDY – Using the workforce properly (page 171)

1. Using the workforce properly, according to Dr Deeley, will make Australian industry truly competitive. Greater commitment will improve performance.
2. Attitudes in the past had viewed employees as a cost rather than as an investment.
3. Dr Deeley probably felt that by suggesting this he might influence the views of others with his ideas and actions.
4. A Human Resources Week would raise public awareness, encourage managers to think carefully about the techniques they use, and provide a forum for ideas.

TASK – page 172

Answers will vary enormously but might include: there will be no one to turn to for advice; lower morale; a feeling that the team had been split up; pressure; not wanting all of the extra responsibility.

TASK – page 173

By taking his management team away for a week, Sir John Harvey-Jones's team was able to decide what it was to do (task), how they should work together (process), and the methods they would use to undertake their responsibilities (action schedule).

CASE STUDY – Howtown Outdoor Education Centre (pages 173/174)

1. It was viewed as important from the onset to give each group responsibilities which would encourage them to develop group values.
2. When building a raft:
   a the task was the raft-building project itself
   b the process involved the group working together
   c the action schedule was how the group organised itself to build the raft.
3. Although the manner in which each individual copes with the nature of the work is clearly important, more and more employers are moving towards group-working principles and look towards how effectively staff can work together in a team.

CASE STUDY – Ignore teamworking at your peril (pages 175/176

1. Many UK companies have ignored the talents of their workers because of tradition, lack of knowledge of other management techniques, suspicion, failure to take team-working seriously, etc.
2. The benefits highlighted by the examples outlined in the study include higher levels of productivity, improvements in quality and service, identification of training needs, a willingness to put the organisation's interests first, etc.
3. a   At Scunthorpe Rod Mill, productivity increased, quality and service improved.
   b   At Penine SCS, employees took on more responsibility, employees linked their efforts to the overall success of the organisation and even postponed a profit-sharing scheme.

TASK – page 181

The agenda should include a title, date, venue, time, apologies, minutes of last meeting, matters arising, entry fees, bar takings, redecoration of the clubhouse, any other business and date of next meeting.

CASE STUDY – Quality circles in management accounting (page 184)

1. After the introduction of quality circles the number of input errors fell by 1.6 per cent.
2. Quality circles contributed to increased morale because of job satisfaction, which arose because of a feeling that employees were making a more positive contribution to the company and that their skills were being more fully utilised.
3. We would expect students to argue that quality circles could be applied to all other parts of the organisation. It might be worth asking them to identify one area and explain why quality circles might help that area. They should be encouraged to think about specific benefits.

CASE STUDY – Management discovers training (pages 185/186)

1. Training is often regarded as a cost rather than as a benefit because it is difficult to quantify the outcome in the short-term.

Section 2 – The Administration

2 Training will make employees feel valued, enable them to develop a career progression and cater for their higher needs.
3 Answers will vary according to priorities.

CASE STUDY – Gaps in training threaten growth (page 186)

1 Answers will vary and could even be based upon the first-hand experiences of some students. This is a useful task to open a discussion.
2 Answers will vary between government and organisations. It should really be discussed as a matter of degree.
3 NVQs have identified a number of levels against which all vocational qualifications can be compared.

CASE STUDY – Problems as opportunities (pages 186/187)

1 Problems were regarded as challenges or opportunities.
2 Answers will vary. Clearly the more realistic the training programme, the better the participants will be able to cope with situations in the workplace.

Supporting Notes for Part C – The Administration

Further areas to explore

Every organisation has its own organisational codes and conventions which relate to its administrative systems. It may be useful to compare the various ways in which organisations approach administrative activities. For example: How does each use IT facilities? What internal communication systems does each have? How do their external communications systems differ? Does group working take place?

Where two contrasting systems exist, it is sometimes very difficult to praise one and condemn another. More often than not they tend to reflect different ways of achieving the same goal with a similar degree of success.

Another area to explore is how to assess the performance of the different administrative systems. This can be quite complex and relates to come of the work covered in Chapter 16 which looks at producing goods and/or services. Some useful areas to look at briefly include:

- economy of administrative systems in terms of materials, technology and manpower
- the overall efficiency of the administrative process
- the design and layout of administrative activities
- the approach to quality in administration
- organisation and methods analysis
- the influence of motivation and reward systems.

Assignment ideas and suggestions

Of all the areas in the book, the three chapters in this section are probably the easiest to integrate together, and the easiest to integrate into other sections. For example, it is not difficult to identify a task which requires communication skills, the use of information technology and which involves people working together. As a result, much of the assignment work may depend upon how well this area is delivered.

One of the problems which many colleges encounter is the use and availability of IT facilities. Whereas the facilities may be available for use with certain of the identified themes, they may not be available for others. One way of overcoming this is to set up a skills workshop where IT facilities are constantly accessible. The scheme of work for the skills workshop should, after the basic skills have been mastered, come from each of the different themes. Students would then be directly identifying IT and other administrative skills and having their development determined by input from other areas.

One assignment idea for this section is the setting up of a group system which, like a quality circle, may be used to provide suggestions and improve activities. The meetings of such a group could be preceded by an agenda and minutes taken. All relevant documentation should make use of IT facilities. This sort of assignment could run throughout the course and be prompted and monitored regularly with different themes and topics. Students should be encouraged to develop both verbal and written communication skills in a forum in which they influence their own outcomes.

It may be possible for students to administer a relevant business activity or excursion of their choice: for example, a visit to a factory, or arranging for a programme of speakers to come into college.

Whichever way the assignment programme is directed, putting students into realistic situations will undoubtedly help them to develop their basic administrative skills, understanding of administrative systems and personable qualities which employers look for.

THE DEMOGRAPHIC TIME-BOMB

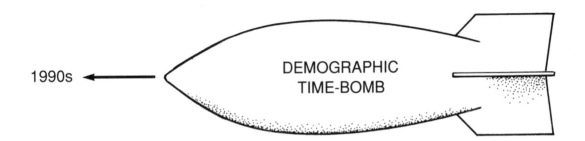

- Dramatic fall in number of 16 – 19 year-olds entering the employment market
- Problems of recruiting suitable young people
- Too many organisations competing for too few people
- Output and quality may be affected
- It may increase pressures upon others
- It will have a demotivating effect.

SOLUTIONS

- Improve motivation
- Maximise contributions from existing employees
- Try to improve retention
- Recruitment of other groups such as women who might have previously stayed at home, disabled, over 50s, long-term unemployed etc.
- Better use of technology.

TEAMWORK

A team is 'a collection of people with a common purpose who communicate with each other over a period of time'. At the very centre of team operation is collaboration.

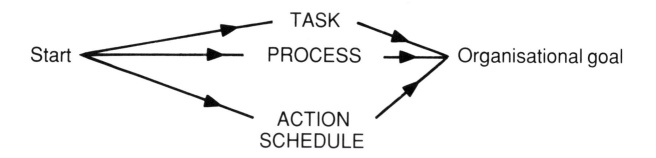

Every team will have 3 elements:
– the task is the content of the work
– the process is the interaction
– the action schedule is how the team is organised.

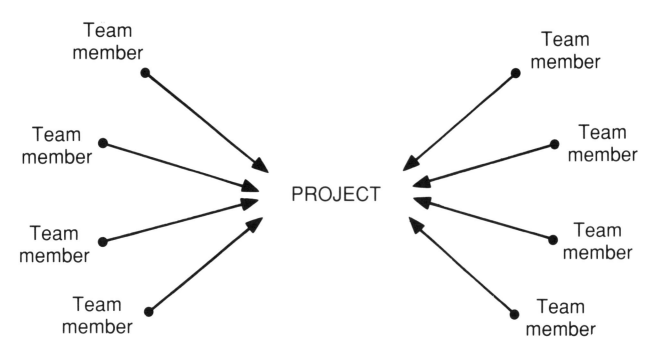

OHP 9.3

GROUP DYNAMICS

For members of a team to work together effectively, it is vital that they understand the corporate objectives of their organisation and how the tasks they are undertaking serve to fulfil such objectives.

Advantages
- can carry out wider range of activities than just an individual
- tasks can be allocated to members
- several heads are better than one
- greater impartiality
- may make more courageous decisions
- sharing of responsibility

Disadvantages
- time may be wasted
- presence of some may inhibit group
- group may be subject to delays
- groups may talk too much and do too little

LEADERSHIP STYLE

If the group leader is <u>autocratic,</u> the group will be driven to agree with the beliefs and goals of the leader.

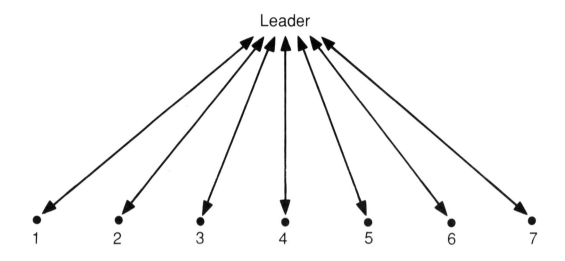

If the group leader is <u>democratic,</u> other members of the group will make extensive contributions to decisions.

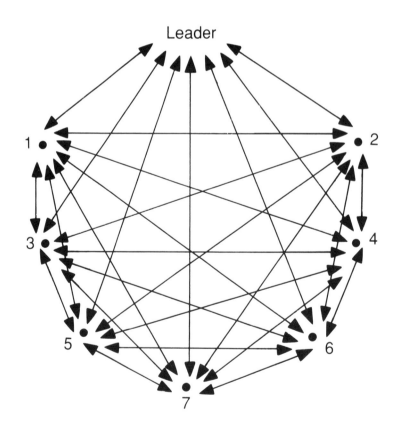

MEETINGS

The purpose of a meeting may be:

- for consultation
- for brainstorming
- to provide information or to spread knowledge
- for negotiation
- to make collective decisions
- to investigate an issue

> A notice of the meeting should specify date, time and place.

> An agenda lists topics to be discussed at the meeting.

A chairperson
- has certain duties and powers
- works through the agenda
- ascertains the views of the meeting

The secretary
- states any apologies
- reads through the minutes of the last meeting
- records the proceedings with a summary of the main points (minutes)

SECTION 2

Part D – Performance

This theme is one of the few where we have dealt almost exclusively with just one area, the financial resources module. We decided to entitle the theme 'performance' because we felt that recording, controlling, monitoring and planning an organisation's finances is inextricably linked to the assessment of the performance of the organisation. Secondly we have adopted, we hope, a much broader approach to financial analysis than many of our predecessors. We have tried to show that by controlling its financial resources an organisation will move towards achieving its objectives. To show this and also highlight other areas, wherever possible, we have used recently researched real and fictitious case studies. We feel that the end result is a slightly more relevant and integrated approach to financial resources which helps to improve and develop each student's understanding of its importance.

Chapter 10 – Financial Resources looks at the need to plan the activities of a business. It starts by assessing what business performance is and how this relates to decisions designed to achieve an organisation's goals and objectives. In forecasting financial requirements, the planning process should assess the various sources of finance, and use cash-flow techniques. As well as the more strategic function of forecasting performance, an organisation should also manage performance on a day-to-day basis, and this involves the setting up of some form of accounting system. Basic financial recording procedures are then assessed.

Chapter 11 – Understanding Financial Statements is concerned with the nature of financial information available for managers in the working environment, and with the need to be able to read and understand financial statements. This chapter looks at the basic statements of a sole trader and then at those of a company. It considers what the statements mean and analyses how they can be interpreted.

Chapter 12 – Using Information for Forecasting is concerned with how organisations use financial information to make decisions. Management accounting provides many of the techniques which enable them to make decisions based upon carefully forecasted results. This chapter looks at the use of capital appraisal techniques, marginal costing, break-even analysis and budgetary control. It concludes by looking at the reasons for business failure.

Chapter 10 Financial Resources

Notes for OHPs

OHP 10.1 *The world of British Airways*
This OHP is designed to assist with the delivery of the Case Study which appears on pages 188 and 189. It provides brief responses to the questions. It is worth emphasising to the students that the purpose of the study is to make them think about why we need to measure and assess performance. The financial information from most organisations is used to assess the extent to which they have achieved a range of objectives.

OHP 10.2 *Sources of finance*
This OHP initially refers to the various sources of finance outlined from pages 190 to 195. Beneath the illustration is a short group activity which can be used to explore the relevance of the various sources of finance to a business idea. Students should be encouraged not only to come up with suggestions about financing Del and Rodney's project, but should also be encouraged to provide ideas about how to take the project further. It should be pointed out to them that to do so would be a planning exercise and that, in order to obtain finance for the project and develop it further, they would have to produce a business plan.

OHP 10.3 *The cash-flow forecast of Albert Spanner*
This OHP provides the answer to the task on page 198 and can be used to go over and check students' responses.

OHP 10.4 *Prime documents*
When transactions take place documents are generated. This OHP refers to the illustration on page 202 and then makes a short definition of some of the stages highlighted.

OHP 10.5 *The cash book of I.M. Lucky Ltd*
This OHP provides the answer to the task which appears on page 206. Beneath the answer students are reminded of the importance of checking the cash column of the cash book and of checking the bank column with the bank statement.

Responses to selected Tasks and Case Studies

TASK – page 190

The drawbacks of bringing a partner into a business can be that disagreements may arise, the partners may still have only limited access to capital, and they will not have limited liability.

CASE STUDY – Burton wins approval for cash call (pages 191/192)

1 Directors have many loyalties to many different parties. Clearly, in this case, the directors' conflict between their own salaries and shareholders' interests are being questioned. They would argue that by providing good remuneration to attract the best people, eventually the company and the shareholders will benefit.
2 'One-for-one' refers to the number of shares offered to each shareholder by the rights issue.
3 Answers to this might vary but would undoubtedly centre on the divided loyalties of the directors.

CASE STUDY – Japanese borrowers (page 193)

1 This is the sort of task that students can be asked to follow up and is particularly relevant to many people's personal finances today. The question asks 'to what extent?'. Students could be asked to explore the issues concerned. For example, were those who borrowed too heavily the ones caught out by the recession? When is it good to borrow and when is it

Financial Resources

unwise to borrow?
2 If an organisation borrows too much, payments and interest may reduce both profitability and liquidity.

TASK – page 194

With leasing, an organisation has neither to save nor to borrow. It can have the goods immediately and, depending on the agreement, the goods might be regularly updated or serviced by the lessor. Their use is paid for by revenue expenditure rather than capital expenditure, and this may leave capital available for other investments.

CASE STUDY – Late payers deal the fatal blow (pages 194/195)

1 Late payments affect liquidity and this may influence the ability of small and medium-sized companies to meet their commitments and continue to trade.
2 By withholding payments the cash position is immediately improved and cash is available for other uses.
3 Answers might vary but most people seem to think about a month.
4 Credit control involves assessing carefully who the organisation is prepared to do business with, the setting of credit limits, the monitoring of credit periods, and trying to get money in on time. In its wider role, the effectiveness of the credit controller will directly influence the cash-flow position of the company.
5 Late payment is causing many small companies to worry about getting money in, and this is directly affecting their ability to compete with similar businesses overseas who do not suffer from the same disadvantage.

CASE STUDY – When the numbers fail to add up (page 196)

1 For suppliers of finance, the ability of an organisation to manage its cash flow and liquidity is often considered to be more important than profitability. This is a good case for bringing this distinction out. Banks consider good cash management important simply because without it many businesses fail.
2 Cash flow enables an organisation to answer hypothetical questions based upon events which may take place during a year, like the loss of a contract, or an increase in bad debts.
3 Many businesses ignore cash flow because of ignorance, over-emphasis upon profits rather than cash, because flows have not been reviewed and updated, because of over-optimism, and sometimes because of investment in speculative projects which take up too much cash.

TASK – page 197

C. Moon Ltd would no longer need overdraft requirements and, at the end of June, the cash balance would now be £5500.

CASE STUDY – The Accounting Standards Board (page 201)

1 SSAPs were constructed to provide a consistency of approach to accounting statements and procedures.
2 The ASC was criticised for failure to respond to emerging issues; lack of timeliness; doubts over independence; concern over flexibility.
3 The independent Accounting Standards Board will set standards in its own right and attempt to meet the criticisms levelled at the ASC.

CASE STUDY – Electronic data interchange (pages 202/203)

1 EDI will provide faster interchange of information, save time and improve communications and efficiency.
2 EDI should reduce lead times and enable suppliers to become more responsive to short-term market needs.
3 EDI might allow others to access the system. It could be open to computer fraud. Mistakes may be difficult to detect. Experts may have to be employed to oversee the system.
4 EDI will be more difficult for smaller suppliers, particularly those with many customers in a horizontal market. The cost of the system and the expertise necessary to maintain it may become a problem.

TASK – page 205

The totals in the daybooks will be as follows:
Sales daybook – £850.69
Purchases daybook – £2016.34
Returns inwards daybook – £15.00
Returns outwards daybook – £102.40.

TASK – page 208

RECEIPTS			PAYMENTS		
DATE	DETAILS	BANK £	DATE	DETAILS	BANK £
30 Sept	Balance b/d	379	16 Sept	Bank transfer	12
04 Sept	Credit transfer	25	24 Sept	Standing order	50
18 Sept	Credit transfer	39	30 Sept	Balance c/d	381
		443			443
30 Sept	Balance b/d	381			

Amended cash book bank columns of C. More Ltd

```
                    G. More Ltd
       Bank Reconciliation Statement as at 30th September 199-
                                                              (£)
Balance at bank as per cash book (amended)                    381
Add:   cheques drawn but not yet presented for payment
         N. Ray           55
         P. Bryan         82
         J. Jewel        151                                  288
Less:  cheques deposited but not yet cleared
         R. Mink                                               58
Balance as per bank statement                                 611
```

CASE STUDY – Beating the cash flow crisis (pages 208/209)

1 Organising cash flow efficiently and successfully is essential for every organisation. Organisations which do not manage cash would not be able to finance their operations.
2 Factoring may mean that other methods of finance are not necessary; organisations do not have to relinquish any control; factoring offers efficient collection of debts; and savings can be made on time and administration costs.
3 Other methods might include: charging interest on overdue debts; employing a credit controller; monitoring credit levels.

OHP 10.1

THE WORLD OF BRITISH AIRWAYS

1. BA's seven goals are:
   - to be safe and secure
   - to have a strong and consistent financial performance
   - to have a leading share of air travel worldwide
   - to provide a superior service
   - to provide good value for money in every market segment
   - to create a working environment which attracts, retains and develops committed employees
   - to be a good neighbour

2. Goals – create shared values/provide direction/enable performance to be assessed.

3. a – it goes through booms and slumps associated with the performance of an economy
   b – their market is worldwide
   c – their market is divided up into smaller markets known as segments
   d – employees are encouraged to share in their successes

4. BA's information systems will provide a guide against which they can assess performance.

5. An overriding objective is one which underpins others. Making profits enables other objectives to be achieved

SOURCES OF FINANCE

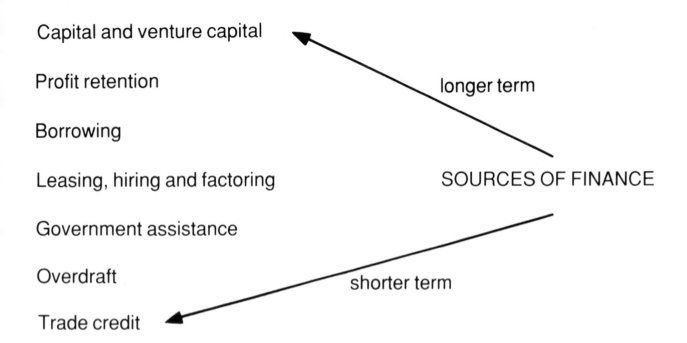

CASE STUDY – the adaptable bike

Del Boynton would describe himself as a rising entrepreneur with a variety of business interests. One of his close contacts, Rodney Trotsky, has recently researched and developed a new type of bicycle which can be built from a kit. It can also be dismantled easily, adapted to different sizes, and parts of it can be used to make, for example, a wheelbarrow, trolley or sledge. Del and Rodney have extensively researched the market and have tested their product. They are convinced of its potential. They are, however, worried about how to finance the project.

TASK – Form small groups. Explore all of the options open to Del and Rodney and report back on your findings. In doing so explain what they must do to take the project further.

OHP 10.3

THE CASH-FLOW FORECAST OF ALBERT SPANNER

	JAN £	FEB £	MAR £	APR £	MAY £	JUNE £
RECEIPTS						
Sales – cash	500	1000	1550	1750	2050	2100
Sales – credit	0	0	1500	3000	4650	5250
Other receipts	0	0	0	0	4000	0
Total receipts	500	1000	3050	4750	10700	7350
PAYMENTS						
Raw Materials	0	0	3200	3350	4185	5500
Wages	800	800	800	800	800	800
Machinery	0	2500	0	0	3500	0
Rent	250	250	250	250	250	250
Other overheads	0	1000	1000	1000	1000	1000
Total payments	1050	4550	5250	5400	9735	7550
Opening balance	17400	16850	13300	11100	10450	11415
Add receipts	500	1000	3050	4750	10700	7350
	17900	17850	16350	15850	21150	18765
Less payments	1050	4550	5250	5400	9735	7550
Balance carried forward	16850	13300	11100	10450	11415	11215

PRIME DOCUMENTS

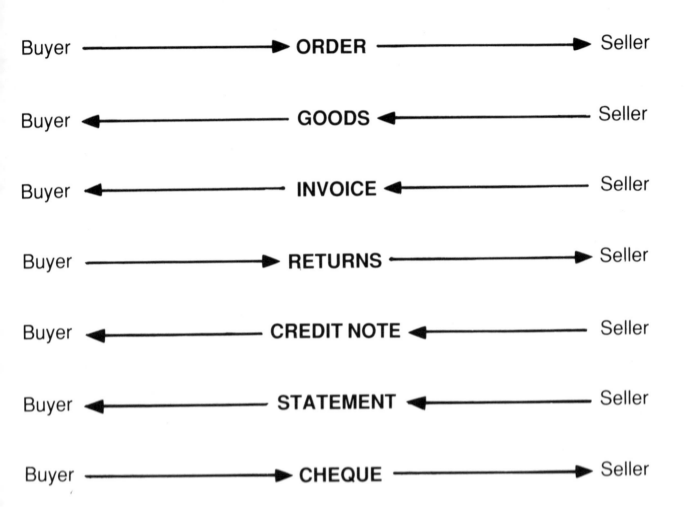

On receipt of an ORDER, a seller will send GOODS to the buyer.

The seller will then issue an INVOICE which will contain all of the details of the transaction.

If the goods are unsatisfactory and have to be returned to the seller, a CREDIT NOTE will be issued by the seller to reduce the invoice total.

If the buyer regularly engages in business with the seller, the buyer may wait for the monthly STATEMENT before making payment. This will detail all of the transactions made.

OHP 10.5

THE CASH BOOK OF I.M.LUCKY LTD

	RECEIPTS				PAYMENTS		
DATE	DETAILS	CASH	BANK	DATE	DETAILS	CASH	BANK
199-		£	£			£	£
1 Aug	Balances b/d	265	1657	3 Aug	Motor expenses		44
2 Aug	Sales	278		7 Aug	Stationery	10	
4 Aug	A. Bennett		125	10 Aug	R. Sid Ltd		76
8 Aug	Sales	400		17 Aug	Bank C	350	
17 Aug	Cash C		350	25 Aug	B. Nasty Ltd		322
22 Aug	A. Pidgeon		65	28 Aug	Wages		476
27 Aug	Sales	30		29 Aug	Stationery	33	
				31 Aug	Balances c/d	580	1279
		973	2197			973	2197
1 Sept	Balances b/d	580	1279				

<u>Checking the cash columns</u> – At the end of every accounting period, the closing balances of the cash book cash columns should be checked with the cash in hand. If the figure does not agree it may be due to an incorrect entry, incorrect totalling, loss or theft of cash or loss of a source document such as a receipt.

<u>Checking the bank columns</u> – The bank columns should be checked against the latest bank statement.

Chapter 11 Understanding Financial Statements

Notes for OHPs

OHP 11.1 *The final accounts of J. O. Nory*
The trading and profit and loss account for the Task on pages 215 and 216 of the text.

OHP 11.2 *The final accounts of J. O. Nory*
The balance sheet. OHPs 1 and 2 can be used to go through the question and to check student responses.

OHP 11.3 *The final accounts of Twyford Ltd*
The trading, profit and loss and appropriation accounts for the Task on pages 219 and 220 of the text.

OHP 11.4 *The final accounts of Twyford Ltd*
The balance sheet.

OHP 11.5 *Accounting ratios*
This OHP lists accounting ratios by the categories which appear in the book between pages 223 and 227. It can be used to go through the formulas for each and to provide a basis upon which to expand your explanations further.

Responses to selected Tasks and Case Studies

CASE STUDY – Assessments and payments of tax (page 212)

1. It is a legal requirement to make a true return of income each year.
2. Keeping accurate records is essential. If they are not kept, the tax assessment may be too high.
3. If a business makes a loss it can be set against: future profits; relief for the same year as the year of loss; relief for income tax for the year following the year of the loss; and relief for the three tax years before that in which the loss is made.
4. Many small businesses worry about income tax arrangements. A small firms advisory service may provide help and support for those thinking of going into business by providing them with specialist advice.

TASK – page 212

Sales of £100 000 less cost of sales £40 000 (10 000 + 50 000 – 20 000) provides a gross profit of £60 000. From the gross profit, total expenses of £20 000 (5000 + 5000 + 10 000) leave a net profit of £40 000.

TASK – page 213

The following order of liquidity will apply for a small bakery:

Fixed assets
the baker's premises
a bakery van
the bakery oven
Current assets
supplies of flour (stocks – raw materials)
bread in the shops (stocks – finished goods)
money in the bakery's bank account
cash in the tills

CASE STUDY – Brand accounting (pages 213/214)

1. Comments will vary, but clearly brands will help to provide a more accurate business valuation. If included in a balance sheet, they would be an intangible fixed asset.
2. Advantages of including brands in the balance sheet might include: a more accurate valuation; they are of long-term benefit to the organisation; stops shares from becoming undervalued. Disadvantages include: it is very difficult to value brands with any precision; brand popularity may constantly change with trends and fashions; they are not usually sold; it is very difficult to turn them into cash.

TASK – page 214

Current assets from the list would include: cash in the tills; money in the bank; money owed by customers for newspaper bills; stocks of newspapers in the shops. (N B The last item might be debated as newspapers are on sale or return.)

TASK – (pages 217/218)

Workhard Ltd's net profit of £300 000 would first have tax deducted at 25 per cent to leave a profit after tax of £225 000. From this would be deducted ordinary dividends of £50 000 and preference dividends of £30 000, to leave £145 000. £50 000 would be deducted from this to leave £95 000. This would be added to the retained profit from the previous year of £125 000 to leave a total balance of retained profit of £220 000 to be transferred to the balance sheet.

TASK – page 222

An investor might require information about profits both past and present, company activities, liquidity, capital structure, other investments, etc. Much of this type of information would normally appear in an annual report.

CASE STUDY – King cash (pages 222/223)

1. Shareholders have a right to be informed. In particular they have a right to a true and fair view of a company's position. Accounting procedures have been considerably maligned over recent years, and so the introduction of cash-flow statements is the first step designed to further protect shareholders' interests.
2. There are many reasons for this. Two of the most important are that many UK accounting practices today have offices overseas, and secondly many companies work on an international basis.
3. Profit is simply a surplus from trading which provides a return on an investment. Cash is more tangible than profit. It is part of the working capital available to pay short-term debts. It is a physical resource available to meet creditors.
4. A business which fails to meet creditors might become liquidated.
5. Cash-flow statements provide more information on liquidity. They will assist shareholders in assessing the risk they are undertaking.

TASK – page 224

They may do this to check against pilfering of stock or to check against cash losses from the till.

Section 2 – Performance

TASK – page 225

- Gross profit percentage – Relates gross profit to sales revenue. The figure has increased, probably as a result of rising prices.
- Net profit percentage – The percentage has fallen marginally between the two years, probably indicating rising costs. (NB See if any students pick up the trick question, as net profit percentage is larger than the gross margin in the first year. This cannot happen.)
- ROCE has fallen, indicating that shareholders are not receiving such a good return on their investment.
- Current ratio has fallen but the acid-test ratio has not, thereby indicating a fall in stocks.

TASK – page 226

Businesses which need to replace stocks regularly may include:
- a newsagent
- a bakery
- a fashion clothes shop
- a cigarette kiosk
- a greengrocer
- a pub.

Businesses which hold on to stock may include:
- a wholesaler
- a music store
- a water company
- a furniture warehouse
- a bookshop
- a jeweller.

Stock costs money both in terms of costs of looking after it and also because if it is not constantly turning over it is not making money.

CASE STUDY – The Maxwell legacy (page 227)

1. If you rely too heavily on loan capital you may be badly affected by rises in interest rates, you will find it difficult to raise new loans, and profits will be squeezed because of the need to repay loan interest.
2. Overtrading involves financing production or expansion with inadequate working capital. For example, in the Maxwell example, the business had expanded so fast that they could not finance its activities without reverting to further loans.

CASE STUDY – Comparing financial statements (page 229)

1. a Jane 25%, Alan 20%.
   b Jane 15%, Alan 12%.
2. Jane's gross margin is 5 per cent higher than Alan's, but her net margin is only 3 per cent higher. This would tend to indicate that Jane has proportionately higher overheads.
3. Alan may increase his working capital by: improving the efficiency of the cash cycle (perhaps by employing a credit controller); any fixed asset not being fully used could be disposed of or rented out; he could review his stock levels and consider economy measures; cash budgeting could be undertaken to improve management of cash; short-term factors could be used – such as an overdraft or bringing in a factoring company.

CASE STUDY – What about quality? (page 229)

1. It is often the first reaction. Cutting costs increases the margin and, as a short-term measure, may quickly bring a company back into profitability.
2. Improved quality will boost the performance of the organisation. It will also alleviate the necessity to cut costs.
3. Quality will reduce waste, elevate the status of employees, add revenues and reduce costs.

OHP 11.1

THE FINAL ACCOUNTS OF J. O. NORY

The trading and profit and loss account of J. O. Nory for the year ended 31 December 1992

	(£)	(£)
Sales		81250
Less cost of sales:		
Opening stock	12700	
Add purchases	18325	
	31025	
Less closing stock	10300	
		20725
GROSS PROFIT		60525
Less expenses:		
Electricity	1451	
Stationery	1526	
Business rate	1845	
Loan interest	3955	
Advertising	2150	
Sundry expenses	1205	
		12132
NET PROFIT		48393

OHP 11.2

THE BALANCE SHEET OF J. O. NORY AT 31 DECEMBER 1992

The balance sheet of J. O. Nory
for the year ended 31 December 1992

	(£)	(£)
Fixed assets		
Land and buildings		161000
Machinery		4900
Motor vehicles		18300
		184200
Current assets		
Stocks	10300	
Debtors	12100	
Bank	4250	
Cash	325	
	26975	
Less **Current liabilities**		
Creditors	4300	
WORKING CAPITAL		22675
		206875
Less **Long-term liabilities**		
Bank loan	10000	
Mortgage	20000	
		30000
		176875
Financed by:		
Capital		137832
Add net profit		48393
		186225
		9350
Less drawings		176875

THE FINAL ACCOUNTS OF TWYFORD LTD

The trading, profit and loss and appropriation account of Twyford Ltd for the year ended 31 December 1992

	(£)	(£)
Sales		123400
Less cost of sales		
Opening stocks	7300	
Add purchases	12500	
	198000	
Less closing stock	3400	
		16400
		107000
GROSS PROFIT		
Less expenses:		
Electricity	4100	
Advertising	3200	
Business rate	800	
Salaries	16000	
Directors' salaries	18000	
Loan interest paid	4400	
Debenture interest paid	1000	
		47500
NET PROFIT		59500
Less Corporation Tax		14875
Profit after tax		44625
Less proposed dividends:		
Ordinary shares	5000	
Preference shares	1000	6000
		38625
Less transfer to General Reserve		3000
		35625
Add retained profit from previous year		4900
Balance of retained profit		40525

BALANCE SHEET OF TWYFORD LTD

The balance sheet of Twyford Ltd as at 31 December 1992

	(£)	(£)	(£)
Fixed assets			
Land and buildings			124000
Motor vehicles			16000
			140000
Current assets			
Stocks		3400	
Debtors		7000	
Bank		15000	
Cash		1000	
		26400	
Less **Current liabilities**			
Creditors	4000		
Proposed dividends:			
Ordinary shares	5000		
Preference shares	1000		
Corporation tax	14875	24875	
WORKING CAPITAL			1525
			141525
Less **Long-term liabilities**			
Bank loan		25000	
10% Debentures		10000	
			35000
			106525
Financed by:			
Authorised share capital:			
50000 ordinary shares £1			50000
10000 preference shares £1			10000
			60000
Issued share capital:			
50000 ordinary shares £1 fully paid			50000
10000 preference shares £1 fully paid			10000
			60000
Reserves			
General reserve		6000	
Balance of retained profit		40525	46525
			106525

ACCOUNTING RATIOS

Profitability

Return on capital employed = $\dfrac{\text{net profit for year}}{\text{capital employed}} \times 100\%$

Gross profit percentage = $\dfrac{\text{gross profit}}{\text{sales revenue}} \times 100\%$

Net profit percentage = $\dfrac{\text{net profit}}{\text{sales revenue}} \times 100\%$

Liquidity

Current or working capital ratio =
current assets : current liabilities

Quick ratio/acid-test ratio/liquidity ratio =
current assets less stock : current liabilities

Debtor's collection period = $\dfrac{\text{debtors}}{\text{average daily sales}}$

Credit period = $\dfrac{\text{creditors}}{\text{average daily purchases}}$

Asset usage

Stock turnover = $\dfrac{\text{cost of sales}}{\text{average stock}}$

Asset utilisation = $\dfrac{\text{sales}}{\text{fixed assets}}$

Capital structure

Gearing = $\dfrac{\text{interest-bearing capital}}{\text{risk capital}}$

Interest cover = $\dfrac{\text{profit before interest and tax}}{\text{interest paid in the year}}$

Section 2 – Performance

Chapter 12 Using Information for Forecasting

Notes for OHPs

OHP 12.1 *West Brighton PLC*
This OHP provides the answers to the Case Study on page 236. The first part illustrated applies each of the capital appraisal techniques to the two projects mentioned in the case, and the answer to the second part indicates other information which may be of value before a decision is made.

OHP 12.2 *Eddie Bowen's break-even chart*
This OHP is simply designed to assist with the teaching of break-even analysis by providing a copy of the chart which appears on page 239. Below this is a definition which can be used as a basis for further research and analysis.

OHP 12.3 *Taking over the family business*
This OHP can be used to go through the answers to the first three tasks of the Case Study on page 240. The OHP provides the break-even point both in number of customers required to make a gross profit of £35 000 and then shows a break-even chart with a break-even point, profit target and margin of safety. Though students could, theoretically, use any form of appraisal for task 4, no mention is made of a rate of discount, though an appropriate level could be provided. The investment is £180 000 and with a profit target of £35 000, the payback would appear after five years, early in year 6. The accounting rate of return would be £35 000, divided by the initial outlay of £180 000 as a percentage and this would be 19.4 per cent. Other information which John Smith might require: demographic; economic; information from the British Tourist Board; market information on actions of competitors.

OHP 12.4 *The budgeting team*
This OHP can be used to introduce budgeting and supports the approach used on pages 242 and 243. It comprises a short illustration beneath which it considers the functions of the budgeting team.

OHP 12.5 *Washington Ltd*
This OHP is simply designed to provide a slightly different approach to marginal costing and can be used to support the work from page 237 to page 240. The OHP provides a short Case Study followed by a short task which asks students to calculate the contribution from each product and the budgeted profit for the next year. The purpose of the task is to help students to relate the marginal costing approach to profit forecasts, without always having to revert to break-even analysis. The answer to the task also appears.

Responses to selected Tasks and Case Studies

CASE STUDY – The need to forecast (pages 231/232)

1. The purpose of this task is to show that, whatever the project, there is always a degree of risk. Students will interpret each task differently and the responses to this task may be used as a basis for discussion. Glaxo's is clearly the safest project and the degree of risk in each of the others is open to debate.
2. The Denver airport project would have required information on: the market; passenger volumes; use of other forms of transport; costs; revenues; environmental considerations; etc. Glaxo would have required information on: competition; patient numbers; product research information; costs; revenues; alternative medicines; etc. Bass required: financial information; market information; information on costs; revenues; economic information; etc.
   Dooley's most important criterion was to identify that a market could be created in East Germany. Information about the market should have been his greatest priority. Other information should have been about transport infrastructure, economic information, knowledge of costs and revenues, political information, etc.
3. The purpose of this task is to enable students to appreciate that information reduces risk.
4. Even though information reduces risk, it can never eliminate it.

TASK – page 233

Project II has shortest payback and provides a payback in year 2.

TASK – page 234

Similarities: both are a form of capital appraisal which considers alternatives; both use similar information; both provide the basis for some form of action; both are simple to calculate.
Differences: one relates a project to a time period, the other relates it to a percentage return; ARR accounts for cash flows, payback does not.

TASK – page 237

```
                                              (£)
Sales revenue (2000 x 9)                   18 000
Less marginal costs (2000 x 5)             10 000
Total contribution                          8 000
Less fixed costs                            4 000
Net profit                                  4 000
```

Units of production	Fixed costs (£)	Variable costs (£)	Total costs (£)	Revenue (£)	Profit (loss) (£)
500	4 000	2 500	6 500	4 500	(2 000)
1 000	4 000	5 000	9 000	9 000	–
1 500	4 000	7 500	11 500	13 500	2 000
2 000	4 000	10 000	14 000	18 000	4 000
2 500	4 000	12 500	16 500	22 500	6 000
3 000	4 000	15 000	19 000	27 000	8 000

Using Information for Forecasting

TASK – page 238

a The break-even point in both units and sales value is: – 1500 units at a sales value of £37500.
b The units and value required to achieve a profit of £18000 are: 3000 units at a sales value of £75000.

CASE STUDY – The born-again IBM (pages 241/242)

1 If the company was to deal with increasing competition and declining margins it had to be leaner and fitter. The Temple Plan involved a series of measures designed to provide a brighter future for the organisation. At the heart of any planning process is the ability to forecast the effects of any measures taken.
2 Budgeting involves taking measures which attempt to make sure that a plan succeeds.
3 This indicates a move towards further market-orientation.
4 The computer model could record budgetary activities, amend forecasts and provide regular details of variances.

TASK – page 246

The balance sheet of R. Salt at 1 January 1992

	(£)	(£)
Fixed assets		
Land and buildings		100 000
Fixtures and fittings		5 000
		105 000
Current assets		
Stocks	1 000	
Bank	14 000	
Working capital		15 000
		120 000
FINANCED BY:		
Capital		120 000
Capital employed		120 000

R. Salt's cash budget

	Jan (£)	Feb (£)	Mar (£)	Apr (£)	May (£)	Jun (£)
Receipts						
Sales cash	2100	1800	1800	2100	1800	2000
Total receipts	2100	1800	1800	2100	1800	2000
Payments						
Purchases of stock	–	–	1400	1200	1700	1800
Wages	400	400	400	400	400	400
Business rate	70	70	70	70	70	70
Insurance	30	30	30	30	30	30
Transport	20	20	20	20	20	20
Advertising	20	20	20	20	20	20
Drawings	600	600	600	600	600	600
Fixtures and fittings	–	–	400	–	–	–
Total payments	1140	1140	2940	2340	2840	2940
Opening bank	14000	14960	15620	14480	14240	13200
Add receipts	2100	1800	1800	2100	1800	2000
	16100	16760	17420	16580	16040	15200
Less payments	1140	1140	2940	2340	2840	2940
Balance c/f	14960	15620	14480	14240	13200	12260

Financial operating statement of R. Salt for six months ended 30 June 1992

	(£)	(£)
Sales		11 600
Less cost of sales		
Opening stock	1 000	
Add purchases	8 500	
	9 500	
Less closing stock	4 300	5 200
Gross profit		6 400
Less expenses:		
Wages	2 400	
Business rate	420	
Insurance	180	
Transport	120	
Advertising	120	3 240
Net profit		3 160

Forecast balance sheet of R. Salt at 30 June 1992

	(£)	(£)
Fixed assets		
Land and buildings		100 000
Fixtures and fittings		5 400
		105 400
Current assets		
Closing stock	4 300	
Bank	12 260	
	16 560	
Less **Current liabilities**		
Creditors	2 400	
working capital		14 160
		119 560
FINANCED BY:		
Capital		120 000
Add net profit		3 160
		123 160
Less drawings		3 600
		119 560

CASE STUDY – The reasons for business failure (page 250)

1 Causes of business failure might include: economic recession; inaccurate forecast; falling market; high interest rates; high gearing; late payments; tough action by the banks; overtrading.
2 Answers might vary widely but include: controlling of cash flow; budgeting; properly appraising projects; basing of forecast on carefully researched information; not overtrading; monitoring costs.
3 The various stages are firstly falling profitability, increased gearing, losses, liquidation, receivership.
4 Answers should be based upon recent examples.

Supporting Notes for Part D – The Performance

Further areas to explore

There are two broads areas within this core module which are capable of further expansion.

Firstly, it is possible to expand and develop the area of personal finance. This is a useful area which can be used to provide students with an early first unit assignment. It can also be used as a basis for developing each section further. For example, they could look at sources of personal finance and then this could be built upon to discover the sources of finance for different types of organisations. Other areas to explore might include an analysis of personal assets and liabilities and the introduction of simple cash flow statements such as that below. (NB It would be useful to record the cash flow work using spreadsheets.)

EXAMPLE – Imagine that you earn £100 a week and have certain fixed weekly expenses. These are: rent to parents £40; daily fares £5; lunches £10; weekends £12; records, magazines £10.

On 1 January you receive your wages of £100. You owe your father £60 from December. A deposit for £30 for a holiday must be paid during the second week of the month. This week there is an extra bill of £11 to see a band playing in York. Assume that there are four weeks in January and in the third week you economise and do not buy any records and magazines. A simple cash flow forecast will enable you to see if you can afford to do all of these things and help you to predict how soon you can pay the loan back to your father.

	1 (£)	2 (£)	3 (£)	4 (£)
Income	100	100	100	100
Expenses:				
Rent	40	40	40	40
Daily fares	5	5	5	5
Lunches	10	10	10	10
Weekends	12	12	12	12
Records, magazines	10	10	-	10
Entertainment	11	-	-	-
Total	88	107	67	77
Net	12	(7)	33	23
Carried forward	12	5	38	61

The loan can be repaid in week 4.

Another area capable of further expansion is that of the presentation of financial statements. In the book we have deliberately limited our analysis to the final accounts of sole traders and limited companies. Other areas to pursue include the final accounts of partnerships, non-profit-making organisations, and local authorities. (NB This information can be obtained from each local authority and analysed individually.)

The following may be useful for developing this area:

1 Partnership statements

The Partnership Act of 1890 defines a partnership as: 'the relation which subsists between persons carrying on in business in common with a view of profit'. It has the following rules:
- Profits and losses should be shared equally between partners.
- No partner should receive a salary.
- Partners are not entitled to receive interest on their capital.
- Interest is not to be charged on partners' drawings.
- If a partner contributes more capital than agreed, he or she can receive interest at 5 per cent a year on the excess.

The above rules must be followed unless the partners agree amongst themselves to follow different guidelines. A partnership agreement may contain the following: details of profit sharing; whether interest is to be charged on capital, and the rate; whether interest is to be charged on drawings, and the rate.

The main differences between the financial statements of a partnership and those of a sole trader are that (1) after the profit and loss account an appropriation section appears which divides the profit between partners, and (2) in the balance sheet, the capital section shows the partners' capital and current account balances. We show here an example of an appropriation account.

	(£)	(£)
Net profit		18 000
Add interest on partners' drawings:		
Smith	1 000	
Jones	2 000	3 000
		21 000
Appropriation of profits		
Salary: Smith		4 000
Interest on partners' capitals:		
Smith	3 000	
Jones	2 000	5 000
Share of residue:		
Smith (60%)	7 200	
Jones (40%)	4 800	12 000
		21 000

In the balance sheet, the capital account of each partner is fixed and only changes if a partner increases or decreases his contribution. The current account balances fluctuate and, to each: share of profit is added; salary is added (if applicable); interest on capital is added; drawings are deducted; interest charged on drawings is deducted. We show here an example of an extract from a balance sheet.

FINANCED BY:			
Capital accounts	(£)	(£)	(£)
Tate		30 000	
Lyle		20 000	50 000
Current accounts	Tate	Lyle	
Opening balances	2 300	3 100	
Add: salary	5 000	-	
interest on capital	3 000	2 000	
share of profit	7 500	2 500	
	17 800	7 600	
Less: drawings	4 000	3 000	
interest on drawings	200	150	
	13 600	4 450	18 050
			68 050

2 Statements for non-profit-making organisations

A non-profit-making organisation is generally a group of individuals who co-operate together to provide some form of activity which is for the benefit of either themselves or others. More often than not, the accounts tend to be referred to as 'club accounts'. Accounting statements include:

Supporting Notes for Part D

- A receipts and payments account which is just a simple version of a cash book. It is normally totalled at the end of the financial year and does not include any accruals or prepayments.
- An income and expenditure account. To a certain extent this mirrors a profit and loss account. It influences most of the items from the receipts and payments account, but excludes any asset purchase which is not part of normal running expenses. It will also include any prepayments, subscriptions adjusted to account for those paid in advance, the contributions from fund raising, and any profits from any activities such as a bar.
- A balance sheet in which there is no capital. Instead, it will have an 'accumulated fund' which is the term used to describe the difference between the total assets and total liabilities. A simple example of a non-profit-making organisation's accounts is shown here.

Crown Green Bowls Club
Receipts and payments account for the year ended 31 December 1992

RECEIPTS	(£)	PAYMENTS	(£)
Bank balance 1 Jan	275	Rent	350
Subscriptions	350	Heating	200
Bar takings	4 400	Bar expenses	1 750
Donations	500	Equipment	550
		Ground maintenance	190
		Bank balance 31 Dec	2 485
	5 525		5 525

Crown Green Bowls Club
Income and expenditure account for the year ended 31 December 1992

EXPENDITURE	(£)	INCOME	(£)
Rent	350	Subs (less £50 prepaid)	300
Heating	200	Profit on bar	2 650
Ground maintenance	190	Donations	500
Excess of income over expenditure	2 710		
	3 450		3 450

Balance Sheet extract of Crown Green Bowls club as at 31 December 1992

FINANCED BY:	(£)
ACCUMULATED FUND	14 800
Add excess of income over expenditure	2 710
	17 510

Assignment ideas and suggestions

Although it is difficult to integrate the teaching of this area fully within other themes, it is very easy to include financial aspects in all assignment work. Financial elements exist in almost any decision-making mechanism in organisations and can be used to support a range of assignment ideas. For example, it may be possible to create a case – fictitious or real – which analyses a series of financial statements from an organisation and assesses how the information from them has, with other information and processes, influenced decision making. Other ideas are:

- using a mini-company to record and present financial statements
- the use of financial information in a business plan
- the use of a computerised accounting package in an assignment
- the use of accounting to develop spreadsheet skills.

OHP 12.1

WEST BRIGHTON PLC

1. *Payback*

	Project I (£)	Project II (£)
Initial outlay	-45000	-45000
Year 1 receipts	+18000	+ 6000
Year 2 receipts	+23000	+12000
Year 3 receipts	+28000	+25000
Year 4 receipts	+12000	+25000

Project I pays back early in year 3 while project II does not pay back until year 4.

Accounting rate of return

	Project I	Project II
Total receipts	+81000	+68000
Profit over 4 years	+36000	+23000
Average annual profit	+ 9000	+ 5750

$$\text{ARR for Project I} = \frac{9000 \times 100}{45000} = 20\%$$

$$\text{ARR for Project II} = \frac{5750 \times 100}{45000} = 12.77\%$$

Discounted cash flow (net present value)

Year	Earnings (£)	Discount factor at 6 per cent	NPV (£)
Project I			
Year 1	18000	0.943	16974
Year 2	23000	0.890	20470
Year 3	28000	0.840	23520
Year 4	12000	0.792	9504
			70468
Project II			
Year 1	6000	0.943	5658
Year 2	12000	0.890	10680
Year 3	25000	0.840	21000
Year 4	25000	0.792	19800
			57138

2 *Other information which might be helpful: information about the market, further information about output and costs, information relating to the business environment such as external factors and actions of competitors.*

OHP 12.2

EDDIE BOWEN'S BREAK-EVEN CHART

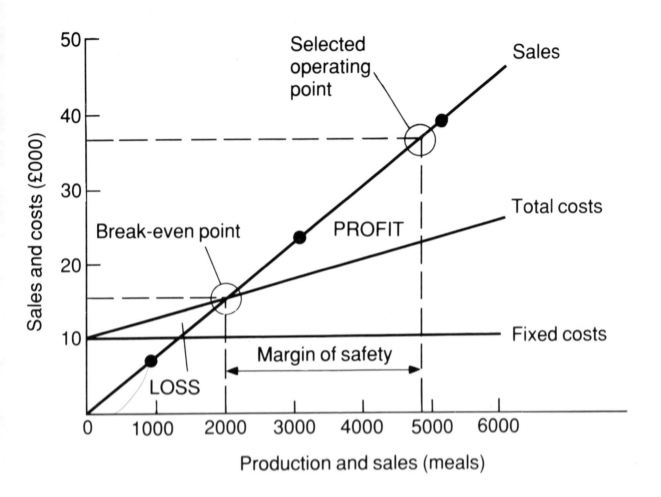

The break-even chart is a simple visual tool enabling managers to anticipate the effects of changes in production and sales upon the profitability of an organisation's activities.

OHP 12.3

TAKING OVER THE FAMILY BUSINESS

Unit contribution = £70 – £20 (£2000/100) = £50 per customer

Break-even point in customers will be:
£107700 (fixed costs) / £50 (unit contribution) = 2154 customers p.a. (roughly 41 customers per week)

The sales value of the hotel at break-even level will be
2154 × £70 = £150780.

The profit target will be achieved by:
£107700 (fixed costs) + £35000 (profit target) =
2854 customers
£50 unit contribution

The margin of safety will therefore be the difference between the selected level of activity and the break-even point. In this example it will be between 2154 and 2854 customers.

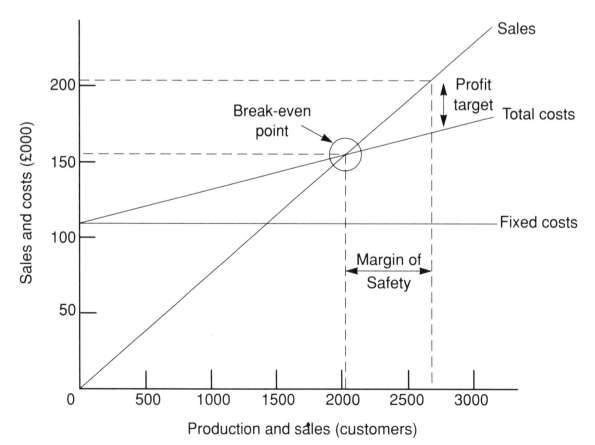

THE BUDGETING TEAM

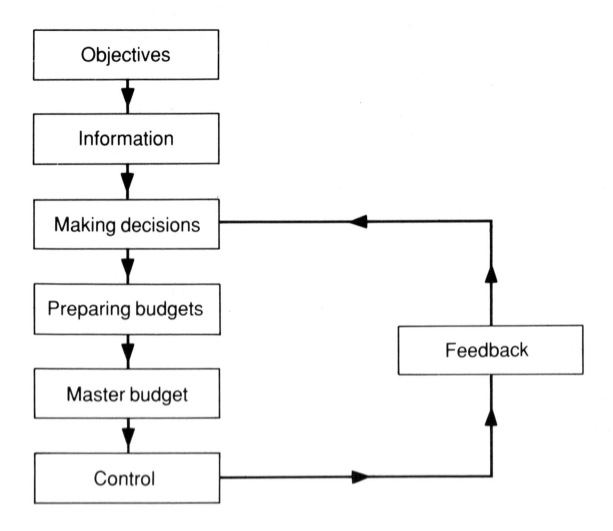

The budgeting team will:
* Consider how the budgets can help the organisation to meet its objectives
* Provide information to base the budget upon.
* Make decisions.
* Prepare budgets for all areas of activity.
* Prepare a master budget to link others together and to forecast a set of final accounts.
* Use budgets as a method of controlling activities and to achieve certain results.

OHP 12.5

WASHINGTON LTD

Washington Ltd produces two high-grade tableware products, known as product A and product B. Each product goes through the same process and uses the same quality of materials. The following apply:

	Product A	Product B
Budgeted sales (units)	1200	3000
Material costs per unit	£8.40	£9.20
labour hours per unit:		
Manufacturing dept	1 hour	$1\frac{1}{2}$ hours
Finishing dept	1 hour	1 hour
Selling price per unit	£26.00	£43.00

Employees in the manufacturing department are paid £3.90 per hour and employees in the finishing department are paid £4.20 per hour.

Budgeted fixed overheads for the year are £22000.

CALCULATE: – The contribution from each product and budgeted profit for the next year.

Answer: Model	Sale price	Variable material	Labour cost	Total unit cost	Contrib. per unit	Prod/sale (units)	Total contribution
A	£26.00	£8.40	£8.10	£16.50	£9.50	1200	£11400
B	£43.00	£9.20	£10.05	£19.25	£23.75	3000	£71250
				Total contribution			82650
				Less fixed costs			22000
				Budgeted profit			60650

STUDENT ACTIVITIES

Given the nature of this area and the need to reinforce each section, we have provided the following 30 student activities. We have also provided brief answers wherever we felt it appropriate to do so.

1. You have decided to go on holiday with a group of friends to EuroDisney. The cost is likely to be around £600 and the only way you can finance your trip is by borrowing.
   a. Comment upon the various options which might be open to you.
   b. Find out what APR stands for.
   c. Try to obtain some publicity material to support some of your options. Comment upon the nature of the loan, e.g. cost, repayment periods etc.
   d. Explain why 'risk' is an important consideration for a provider of finance.

2. At the age of 50, B. Charterhouse has taken early retirement from the bank. He wishes to set up a small business restoring and selling antiquarian books, which has been a hobby of his for many years. Comment upon:
   a. the type of information he should include in his business plan
   b. the possible sources of finance for the business
   c. commercial organisations which might be able to assist him
   d. the type of business organisation he should set up and why.

3. Calculate your own cash-flow forecast for the next month. Wherever necessary break down your payments and receipts.

4. R. Chase intends to set up his business on 1 March. At that time he expects to have £420 in the bank. Over the following 6 months his receipts are likely to be:

Mar	Apr	May	Jun	Jul	Aug
£1400	£1300	£1210	£1298	£1256	£1500

   At the same time his payments are likely to be as follows:

Mar	Apr	May	Jun	Jul	Aug
£1250	£1800	£1560	£1475	£1245	£1700

   a. Construct a cash-flow forecast.
   b. Explain why R. Chase should amend his cash-flow forecast each month with the actual amounts recorded.
   c. What would happen to the final balance if the receipts from April to August were 10% higher than expected (to the nearest pound)?

5. Rachel Took sets up in business on 1 January by putting £15 000 into a business bank account. Her research for the next 6 months indicates that:
   - forecasts for the purchase of raw materials and income from the sale of finished goods are as follows:

	Purchases (£)	Sales (£)
January	5 400	8 900
February	5 700	8 700
March	6 800	10 570
April	6 000	11 000
May	9 000	12 300
June	9 800	14 000

   - suppliers are happy to provide 2 months' credit
   - sales will be one half for cash and one half on credit – she anticipates that on average 1 month's credit will be taken by credit customers
   - wages will be £1000 per month

Section 2 – Performance

- equipment will be purchased in April costing £3400 – payment for the equipment will have to be made in June
- rent is to be £1550 per calendar month
- in April she should receive £5000 from a relative which she intends to put into the business
- other overheads should be £600 per month.

a Prepare Rachel's cash-flow forecast for the 6 months.
b Explain briefly the benefits of constructing such a forecast.

6 Obtain a copy of an invoice used by a business.
  a Explain the purpose of the invoice.
  b Why should invoices be sent out promptly?
  c Design an invoice for a business. Put on it the following details:
    Robin Hood Shoes Ltd of 5 Scarlet Street, West Butterknowle, has ordered the following:
    7 pairs of children's shoes at £9.00 each
    8 pairs of men's shoes at £15.00 each
    VAT is to be charged at the current rate. The invoice number is 4873 and date for today.

7 You work in the accounts office of Paint-A-Lot Ltd and have been asked to enter the following into the appropriate day books:

1 May Invoice 324 sent to PRM Ltd for	£345.00
2 May Invoice 264 received from EJB Ltd for	£675.98
3 May Invoice 145 sent to RDC Ltd for	£134.89
4 May Invoice 465 received from TCP Ltd for	£112.00
5 May Credit Note 378 sent to PRM Ltd for	£15.00
6 May Credit Note 456 received from EJB Ltd for	£25.00
7 May Invoice 367 sent to PRM Ltd for	£800.00
8 May Invoice received from RDG Ltd for	£124.88
9 May Credit Note 455 sent to PRM Ltd for	£21.50

  a Total the day books.
  b Explain how the entries into each day book affect accounts in the ledger.

8 Prepare the cash book of R. Hammer Ltd from the following details:
  1 May   Balances £125. 89 cash, £1800.50 bank
  2 May   Receive £190.00 cash from sales
  3 May   Transfer £150 cash to bank
  4 May   Pay rent £200.00 by cheque
  5 May   Receive £250.88 cheque from B. Body
  6 May   Payment for stationery £10.50 cash
  7 May   Pay wages £75.00 cash
  8 May   Receive £525.00 cash from sales
  9 May   Bank £500 cash
  10 May   Send cheque to R. Tool for £450
  11 May   Pay motor expenses £34.50 by cheque
  12 May   Receive cheque from A. Smarty for £100.00

9 Find out about the services which banks offer their customers:
  a Obtain leaflets which outline the various student services on offer.
  b Make a list of such services.
  c How will the services you have listed help students to improve the ways in which they manage their finances?
  d Compare the services banks offer students with the services banks offer other customers, e.g. personal customers and businesses.

10 Use the bank columns of the cash book of R. Speke and her bank statement covering the same period to prepare a bank reconciliation statement.

The cash book bank columns of R. Speke

RECEIPTS			PAYMENTS		
DATE 1993	DETAILS	BANK (£)	DATE	DETAILS	BANK (£)
1 Jun	Balance b/d	825	2 Jun	R. Pain Ltd	85
4 Jun	M. Peters	50	3 Jun	H. Royce	220
5 Jun	E. Rogers	100	7 Jun	R. Backhouse	400
6 Jun	M. Turner	53	8 Jun	M. Blenkinsop	150
			8 Jun	Balance c/d	173
		1028			1028
8 June	Balance b/d	173			

The bank statement of R. Speke

DATE 1993	DETAILS	PAYMENTS (£)	RECEIPTS (£)	BALANCE (£)
1 Jun	Balance b/d			825
2 Jun	Credit transfer		30	855
2 Jun	R. Pain Ltd	85		770
3 Jun	H. Royce	220		550
4 Jun	Credit		50	600
5 Jun	Standing order	125		475
6 Jun	Credit		100	575
7 Jun	R. Backhouse	400		175
8 Jun	Bank transfer	10		165

11 From the following trial balance of J. Oliver, a sole trader, draw up her trading and profit and loss account for the year ended 31 December 1993, together with her balance sheet as at that date. Her stocks at 31 December 1993 were valued at £18 525.

	(£)	(£)
Stocks 1 Jan 1993	12 414	
Sales		95 250
Purchases	31 330	
Wages	4450	
Electricity	500	
Business rate	1500	
Loan interest	550	
Advertising	150	
Sundry expenses	425	
Land and buildings	125 000	
Fixtures and fittings	5 500	
Motor vehicles	4300	
Debtors	5 306	
Bank	2 550	
Cash	175	
Bank loan		5 000
Mortgage		10 000
Creditors		8 300
Drawings	4 400	
Capital @ 1 Jan 1993		80 000
	198 550	198 550

Section 2 – Performance

12 From the trial balance of L. Nut, a sole trader, draw up the trading and profit and loss account for the year ended 31 December 1993, together with the balance sheet as at that date. His stocks at 31 December 1993 were valued at £4840.

	(£)	(£)
Stocks 1 Jan 1993	15 300	
Sales		81 320
Purchases	35 252	
Wages and salaries	5 750	
Electricity	2 000	
Business rate	1 335	
Loan interest	1 200	
Advertising	550	
Sundry expenses	1 000	
Land and buildings	74 000	
Fixtures and fittings	3 500	
Machinery	4 200	
Motor vehicles	1 750	
Debtors	8 253	
Bank	2 780	
Cash	150	
Bank loan		20 000
Mortgage		10 000
Creditors		8 400
Drawings	12 700	
Capital @ 1 Jan 1993		50 000
	169 720	169 720

13 Denise Williams and Peter Storey are in business selling computer software. They share profits and losses 60% and 40% respectively. Complete their trading, profit and loss and appropriation account for the end of the year from the following trial balance. Prepare a balance sheet at the same date.

	(£)	(£)
Stocks 1 Jan 1993	15 425	
Sales		87 425
Purchases	14 550	
Wages	2700	
Electricity	450	
Rates	1 000	
Stationery	50	
Advertising	825	
Travelling expenses	500	
Sundry expenses	250	
Land and buildings	102 500	
Furniture and fittings	4 500	
Motor vehicles	8 000	
Debtors	145	
Bank	2 400	
Cash	420	
Bank loan		5 000
Creditors		3 790
Capital accounts: D. Williams		45 000
P. Storey		30 000
Current accounts: D. Williams		1 400
P. Storey		1 100
Drawings: D. Williams	10 000	
P. Storey	10 000	
	173 715	173 715

Notes at 31 December 1993:
- stocks are valued at £14500
- Interest on drawings is to be charged at 5%
- Interest on capital is to be allowed at 10%
- D. Williams is to be credited with a salary of £5000

14 P. Pepper and R. Salt are in business selling stationery and share profits equally. Complete their trading, profit and loss and appropriation account for the year ended 31 December 1993. Prepare a balance sheet at that date.

	(£)	(£)
Stocks 1 Jan 1993	18 433	
Sales		42 350
Purchases	11 420	
Wages	3 000	
Electricity	570	
Rates	400	
Advertising	3 100	
Sundry expenses	400	
Land and buildings	25 000	
Furniture and fittings	2 500	
Motor vehicles	1 500	
Debtors	3 000	
Bank	5 172	
Cash	855	
Bank loan		10 000
Creditors		2 500
Capital accounts: P. Pepper		10 000
R. Salt		18 000
Current accounts: P. Pepper		3 000
R. Salt		2 500
Drawings: P. Pepper	5 000	
R. Salt	8 000	
	88 350	88 350

Notes at 31 December 1993
- Stocks are valued at £18300
- Interest on drawings is to be charged at 5%
- Interest on capital is to be allowed at 10%
- P. Pepper is to be credited with a salary of £5000.

15 From the trial balance of Warnock Ltd shown below and the notes which follow it, prepare the trading, profit and loss and appropriation account for the year ended 31 December 1993 and also a balance sheet as at that date.

	(£)	(£)
Stock at 1 January 1993	16 300	
Sales		84 240
Purchases	18 750	
Advertising	4 400	
Wages	14 000	
Stationery	3 200	
Business rate	1 200	
Loan interest paid	900	
Debenture interest paid	1 000	
Sundry expenses	1 000	
Directors' salaries	20 000	
Land and buildings	110 000	
Machinery	6 000	
Debtors	4 700	
Bank	3 090	
Cash	800	
Bank loan		9 000
10% debentures		10 000
Creditors		4 000
General reserve		2 000
Retained profit @ 31 December 1992		16 100
Issued and authorised share capital:		
70 000 ordinary shares of £1		70 000
10 000 preference shares of £1		10 000
	205 340	205 340

Notes at 31 December 1993
- Stocks were valued at £12500
- Corporation tax is to be charged at 25% of profits
- A 12% dividend on ordinary shares is to be paid.
- Preference dividends are to be paid.
- £1000 is to be transferred to the General Reserve.

16 From the trial balance of ABCDE Ltd shown below and the notes which follow it, prepare the trading, profit and loss and appropriation account for the year ended 1 December 1993 and also a balance sheet as at that date.

	(£)	(£)
Stock @ 1 Jan 1993	8 450	
Sales		161 300
Purchases	48 420	
Electricity	4 000	
Wages	9 500	
Stationery	5 000	
Business rate	1 200	
Loan interest paid	1 000	
Debenture interest paid	500	
Directors' salaries	34 000	
Sundry expenses	15 225	
Land and buildings	100 000	
Machinery	25 000	
Fixtures and fittings	8 200	
Debtors	4 300	
Bank	14 567	
Cash	1 288	
Bank loan		10 000
10% debentures		5 000
Creditors		6 350
General Reserve		3 500
Retained profit @ 31 December 1992		4 500
Issued and authorised share capital:		
80000 ordinary shares of £1		80 000
10000 10% £1 preference shares		10 000
	280 650	280 650

Notes at 31 December 1993
- Stocks were valued at £8150
- Corporation tax is to be charged at 25% of profits
- A 15% dividend on ordinary shares is to be paid
- Preference dividends are to be paid
- £2000 is to be transferred to General Reserve.

17 Many people act as unpaid officials for a whole range of clubs and societies. Write a brief written report in answer to the following.
   a Why do people undertake such positions of responsibility?
   b Why should clubs and societies keep accurate records?
   c What is the extent to which club accounts are:
      i) similar to
      ii) different from
      the accounts of a small business such as a sole trader.

Section 2 – Performance

18 The following opening balances were extracted from the books of Greengrass Lawn Tennis club on 1 January 1993:

Land and buildings	50 000
Equipment	3 300
Investments	4 200
Subscriptions – in advance for 1993	200
– in arrears for 1992	50
Bar stock	3 800
Cash in hand and at bank	3 000

Over 1993 the following transactions took place:

RECEIPTS	(£)	PAYMENTS	(£)
Subscriptions	12 800	Ground maintenance	3 100
Bar takings	24 200	Bar expenses	17 400
Interest received	420	Electricity	480
Donations	850	Sundry expenses	2 100
		Equipment	1 000

At the end of 1993 the following balances appeared in the books:

Creditors for bar supplies	£1100
Subscriptions – in advance for 1994	£120
– in arrears for 1993	£80
Bar stocks were valued at	£4100

Prepare an income and expenditure account for the club for the year ended 31 December 1993 and a balance sheet as at that date.

19 You have recently been appointed as treasurer of the Bognor Bingo Society. The previous year's accounts show only a receipts and payments account as follows:

The receipts and payments account for the Bognor Bingo Society for the year ended 31 December 1993

RECEIPTS	(£)	PAYMENTS	(£)
Bank balance 1/1/93	310	Rent	850
Subscriptions	8400	Entertainment	3588
Donations	520	Printing	975
Ticket sales	440	Sundry expenses	1342
Raffles	965	Food and drink	2150
		Bank 31/12/93	1730
	10 635		10 635

At the end of the year your predecessor had noted that:
- £95 of the subs included in the £8400 were paid in advance for 1994
- that the stock of food and drink left over was valued at £350.

Prepare an income and expenditure account for the year and a balance sheet as at that date.

20 The following figures have been extracted from the accounts of Consular Contractors for their first 2 years' trading.

Profit and Loss accounts	Year 1 (£)	Year 2 (£)
Sales	35 200	43 500
Less cost of sales	16 700	21 300
Gross profit	18 500	22 200
Less overheads	6 400	6 450
Net profit	12 100	15 750
Less dividends	8 000	10 000
	4 100	5 750
Add retained profit brought forward		4 100
Balance of retained profit	4 100	9 850

Balance sheets	Year 1 (£)	Year 1 (£)	Year 2 (£)	Year 2 (£)
Fixed assets		18 200		24 700
Current assets				
Stocks	2 300		3 400	
Debtors	1 250		1 350	
Bank	650		700	
	4 200		5 450	
Less current liabilities				
Creditors	3 000		5 000	
Working capital		1 200		450
		19 400		25 150
Financed by:				
Ordinary shares		15 300		15 300
Reserves		4 100		9 850
		19 400		25 150

Prepare and comment upon the following ratios:
a gross profit percentage
b net profit percentage
c current ratio
d quick ratio
e asset utilisation

21 a Make a list of the dangers of using ratios.
 b What information other than ratios would help to provide a more realistic picture of an organisation's performance?
 c Obtain a company's annual report. Using ratio analysis, provide a brief financial summary of the organisation's performance. Comment generally upon their other activities highlighted by the report.

22 Obtain a copy of the annual report and accounts of your local council.
 a Comment upon the extent to which these accounts are
   i) similar to
   ii) different from
   the accounts of a limited company.
 b Use some form of graphical presentation (package) to show the sources of income and expenditure of your local authority.
 c How would the role of the public sector accountant differ from the role of an accountant in the private sector?

Section 2 – Performance

23 Identify which of the following costs are variable and which are fixed:
- raw materials
- factory labour
- office salaries
- rent of premises
- factory power
- business rate.

24 A former colleague of yours has recently started her own business. She is about to make a major investment in plant and machinery and has approached you for advice upon how to appraise properly the alternatives open to her. Using a report format comment upon:
- the need for appraisal techniques and what they achieve
- the merits of each appraisal technique open to her
- other element of possible importance which ought to be considered before she makes any investment decision.

25 Mr Ron Tedd wishes to decide between 2 projects for which he anticipates the following cash flows:

Year	Project A (£)	Project B (£)
0	(50 000)	(50 000)
1	8 000	15 000
2	9 000	15 000
3	10 000	20 000
4	15 000	10 000
5	28 000	10 000

Calculate the payback period for each project and comment upon the figures.

26 Peter Saunders has the choice of buying 1 of 2 shops as a going concern. His accountant forecasts:

	Project A (£)	Project B (£)
Initial outlay	120 000	160 000
Pre-tax profits are likely to be: Year 1	45 000	52 000
Year 2	53 000	65 000
Year 3	60 000	75 000
Year 4	65 000	80 000

Using the accounting rate of return, comment upon the profitability of each project.

27 Thames Valley Holidays Ltd is a small private company which specialises in providing holidays for adults who require a unique form of entertainment. As a result, all of its holidays are based upon a theme. For example, steam railway holidays in China, surf-boarding in America, gourmet breaks in France etc. Thames Valley Holidays is currently reviewing its plans for 1994.

The company anticipates that its fixed overheads will be £900 000 for the year. One half of the packages are likely to be short breaks and one half will be full packages and the company expects to sell 4000 holidays during the year.

With the short breaks, one half of the variable costs goes in travel costs at an average of £35 per package. The company anticipates selling short break packages at an average of £220 each.

The full packages are sold at an average price of £770 per package. Travel costs of £60 comprise one quarter of the variable costs of the holiday.
a   Work out the average contribution of each short break and full package.
b   Calculate the company's profit for the year before tax.
c   Market research has revealed that if Thames Valley Holidays reduced prices by 20% it could sell 400 more holidays. Calculate how this might affect profitability and advise accordingly.
d   Suggest 2 alternative strategies that Thames Valley Holidays could use to increase profitability.

28 Clean-em-up Ltd have benefited enormously from the recession. As companies drive to cut costs, many turn to contracted business services in a process of hiving off non-core activities. Clean-em-up provide cleaning services and have responded rapidly to this growth with a substantial expansion programme.

At present their annual fixed costs are as follows:

	(£)
loan repayment and interest	500 000
rent and rates	125 000
insurance	70 000
staff salaries	95 000
other fixed overheads	150 000
advertising	50 000

The average contract size for Clean-em-up is £15 000 per annum and they expect to increase their number of contracts for the forthcoming year to 190. Each contract will cost them at least £6000 in direct labour and at least £2000 in direct materials. Other variable overheads will be about £500.
a   Work out the break-even point for Clean-em-up in terms of value and volume.
b   Draw a break-even chart to illustrate the above.
c   How much profit will they make with 190 contracts?
d   Given the nature of their investment Clean-em-up wish to make £400 000 profit for the year. How many contracts would they have to acquire to achieve this?
e   One strategy they propose is to increase their advertising budget to £150 000. Research has indicated that increasing the budget to that level will enable them to achieve at least 25 more contracts. How will this affect profitability?

29 Working in a small group:
- decide upon a product or service you feel that you could produce
- decide upon a pricing strategy and agree upon a price
- calculate your fixed overheads
- calculate your variable costs
- estimate how many of these products or services you might be able to sell.

Work out the break-even point in terms of both volume and value and assess the potential profitability of the project. Using various forms of visual aids, make a presentation to other members of your class/group outlining the possibilities for your venture.

30 Find out about the financial information generated in your institution and how it is used by managers. Arrange an interview/talk with the accountant, bursar or administrator or ask one of them to come and speak to the group. Prepare a series of questions in readiness for the interview or meeting. Find out:
- how information is recorded and generated
- who uses the system
- how information technology improves the use of the system
- about costing procedures etc.

Section 2 – Performance

Answers to student activities

1 **a** Personal loans from banks, building societies or finance houses, extended credit on credit cards etc.
  b Annual Percentage Rate.
  d Wherever a loan is made there is a degree of risk involved. The degree of risk may depend upon the character or ownership of other assets.

2 **a** Information would include a description of the idea, details of the business and about the organisation, information about the market, a marketing plan, information about costings and finance.
  b Borrowing, trade credit, venture capital etc.
  c Banks, 3i and other venture capital companies, merchant banks etc.
  d Sole trader, partnership, private limited company etc.

4 **a** The forecast finishes with an overdraft of £646.
  b So that current or recent activities can be used to provide more accurate updated projections.
  c £11 would be left over.

5 **a** The cash-flow forecast would be as follows:

	Jan (£)	Feb (£)	Mar (£)	Apr (£)	May (£)	Jun (£)
Opening balance	15 000	16 300	21 950	23 035	29 970	31 670
Add receipts	4 450	8 800	9 635	15 785	11 650	13 150
	19 450	25 100	31 585	38 820	41 620	44 820
Less payments	3 150	3 150	8 550	8 850	9 950	12 550
Balance carried forward	16 300	21 950	23 035	29 970	31 670	32 270

  b The forecast will help Rachel to manage both her cash and her working capital.

6 **a** The invoice is the most important document in a transaction as it states the goods and terms supplied as well as the amount to be paid by the buyer.
  b If an invoice is not sent promptly it may delay payment.
  c The total transaction is £183 + VAT at 17.5% of £32.02 = £215.02.

7 **a** Sales daybook =   £1280.49
   Purchases daybook =   £912.86
   Returns inwards daybook = £36.50
   Returns outwards daybook = £25.00
  b Sales daybook entries are transferred to the sales account in the general ledger and also to the debtors accounts in the sales ledger.
   Purchases daybook entries are transferred to the purchases account in the general ledger and also to the creditors accounts in the purchases ledger.
   The total for the returns inwards daybook is transferred to the returns inwards account in the general ledger and debtor accounts are adjusted in the sales ledger.
   The total for the returns outwards daybook is transferred to the returns outwards account in the general ledger and creditor accounts are adjusted in the purchases ledger.

8 Balances in the cash book are £105.39 cash and £2116.88 bank.

10 Amended cash book bank columns of R. Speke

RECEIPTS			PAYMENTS		
Date	Details	Bank	Date	Details	Bank
1993		(£)			(£)
8 Jun	Balance b/d	173	5 Jun	Standing order	125
2 Jun	Credit transfer	30	8 Jun	Bank transfer	10
			8 Jun	Balance c/d	68
		203			203
8 Jun	Balance b/d	68			

Bank reconciliation statement of R. Speke as at 8 June 1993

	(£)
Balance as per cash book (amended)	68
Add: cheques drawn but not yet presented for payment – M. Blenkinsop	150
	218
Less: cheques deposited but not yet cleared – M. Turner	53
Balance as per bank statement	165

11 Sales £95 250 less cost of sales £25 219 = gross profit £70 031
less expenses of £7575 = net profit £62 456.
Total fixed assets £134 800 plus working capital £18 256 = £153 056
less long-term liabilities £15 000 = £138 056.
Capital £80 000 + net profit £62 456 = £142 456 less drawings £4400 = £138 056.

12 Sales £81 320 less cost of sales £45 712 = gross profit £35 608
less expenses of £11 835 = net profit £23 773.
Total fixed assets £83 450, plus working capital £7623 = £91 073
less long-term liabilities £30 000 = £61 073.
Capital £50 000 + net profit £23 773 = £73 773 less drawings £12 700 = £61 073.

13 Sales £87 425 less cost of sales £15 475 = gross profit £71 950
less expenses of £5775 = net profit £66 175
plus interest on drawings £1000 = £67 175
less salary D. Williams = £62 175
less interest on capitals £7500 = £54 675.
Share of residue, D. Williams £32 805 and P. Storey £21 870.
Total fixed assets £115 000 plus working capital £13 675 = £128 675
less long-term liability £5000 = £123 675.
Capital account D. Williams £45 000 plus P. Storey £30 000 = £75 000
plus current account D. Williams (1400 + 5000 + 4500 + 32 805 – 10 500) £33 205
plus current account P. Storey (1100 + 3000 + 21 870 – 10 500) £15 470 = £123 675.

14 Sales £52 350 less cost of sales £21 553 = gross profit £30 797
less expenses of £7470 = net profit £23 327
plus interest on drawings £650 = £23 977
less salary P. Pepper = £18 977
less interest on capitals £3800 = £15 177.
Share of residue, P. Pepper £7588.50 and R. Salt £7588.50.
Total fixed assets £39 000 plus working capital £24 827 = £63 827
less long-term liability £10 000 = £53 827.
Capital account P. Pepper £20 000 + R. Salt £18 000 = £38 000
plus current account P. Pepper (3000 + 5000 + 2000 + 7588.50 – 5250) £12 338.50
plus current account R. Salt (2500 + 1800 + 7588.50 – 8400) £3488.50 = £53 827.

Section 2 – Performance

15 Sales £84240 less cost of sales £22550 = gross profit £61690
less expenses of £45700 = net profit £15990
less Corporation Tax of £3997.50 = profit after tax of £11992.50
less dividends (pref £1000 + ordinary £8400) £9400 = £2592.50
less transfer to General Reserve of £1000 = £1592.50
add retained profit of £16100 = £17692.50 as balance to be transferred to the balance sheet.
Fixed assets of £116000 plus working capital £3692.50 = £119692.50
less long-term liabilities £19000 = £100692.50.
Financed by shares of £80000 + reserves of £20692.50 = £100692.50.

16 Sales £161300 less cost of sales £48720 = gross profit £112580
less expenses of £70 425 = net profit £42155
less Corporation Tax of £10538.75 = profit after tax of £31616.25
less dividends (pref. £1000 + ordinary £12000) £13000 = £18616.25
less transfer to General Reserve of £2000 = £16616.25
add retained profit of £4500 = £21116.25 to be transferred to the balance sheet.
Fixed assets of £133200 plus working capital (£1583.75) = £131616.25
less long-term liabilities £15000 = £116616.25.
Financed by shares of £90000 plus reserves of £26616.25 = £116616.25.

18 Accumulated Fund 1 Jan 1993 = £64150 (£50000 + £3300 + £4200 + £50 + £3800 + £3000 − £200)
Surplus of income over expenditure = £14200, comprising income: subs £12910 (£200 − £50 − £120 + £80) + £24200 + £420 + £850 = £38380, less expenditure: £3100 + £18500 (£17400 + £1100) + £480 + £2100 = £24180.
Fixed assets £58500 (£50000 + £4300 + £4200) + current assets £21070 (£3800 + £80 + £17190) = £79570.
Accumulated Fund £64150 plus surplus £14200 = £78350 plus current liabilities (£1100 + £120) £1220 = £79570.

19 Surplus of income over expenditure = £1325, comprising income: subs £8305 (£8400 − £95) + £520 + £440 + £965 = £10230, less expenditure: £850 + £3588 + £975 + £1342 + £2150 = £8905.
Total assets £2080 (£1730 + £350) less subs in advance £95 = £1985 Accumulated Fund.

20 a Year 1 = 52.56%, year 2 = 51.03% – the gross profit percentage remains roughly similar. The slight fall may be due to rising costs of raw materials, stock losses, or thefts.
  b Year 1 = 34.37%, year 2 = 36.2% – the net profit percentage has increased slightly indicating an increase in expenses.
  c Year 1 = 1:1.4, year 2 = 1:1.09 – the current ratio has fallen and, given the size of stocks, would indicate cause for concern.
  d Year 1 = 1: 0.63, year 2 = 1: 0.41 – neither indicates an ability to meet creditors quickly and the position worsens significantly between the 2 years.
  e Year 1 = 1:1.9, year 2 = 1:1.76 – fixed assets are less efficient in generating sales in the second year.

23
- raw materials – variable
- factory labour – variable
- office salaries – fixed
- rent of premises – fixed
- factory power – variable
- business rate – fixed

25 The payback for Project A is in year 5 and for Project B at the end of year 3. The cash flows from the 2 projects differ widely.

26 The ARR for Project A is 46.46% and for Project B is 42.5%.

27 a Short breaks: £220 − £70 = £150
Full packages: £770 − £240 = £530

b
	(£)
2000 × 150 =	300 000
2000 × 530 =	1 060 000
	1 360 000
Less fixed overheads	900 000
Profit	460 000

c New price for short breaks £176
New price for full packages £616
Contribution short breaks = £176 − £70 = £106
Contribution full packages = £616 − £240 = £476

	(£)
2200 × £106 =	233 200
2200 × £476 =	1 047 200
	1 280 400
Less fixed overheads	900 000
Profit	380 400

Profit falls by £79 600 with the alternative proposals.

28 a total fixed overheads = £990 000
Variable costs per contract = £8500
Contribution = £15 000 − £8500 = £6500 per contract

$$\text{BEP} = \frac{990\,000}{6500} = 152 \text{ contracts (to the nearest contract)}$$

Sales value = 152 × £15 000 = £2 280 000

c *190 contracts*

Sales	Fixed overheads	Variable overheads	Total costs	Profit
2 850 000	990 000	1 615 000	2 605 000	245 000

d $\frac{990\,000 + 400\,000}{6500} = \frac{1\,390\,000}{6500} = 214$ contracts (to the nearest contract)

e Fixed overheads increase to £1 090 000

215 contracts

Sales	Fixed overheads	Variable overheads	Total costs	Profit
3 225 000	1 090 000	1 827 500	2 917 500	307 500

The strategy has increased profitability by £62 500.

SECTION 2

Part E – The Wider Business Environment

In this section we set out to explore the background against which every organisation has to operate. Organisations operate within a framework of interlinking systems and dynamic interrelationships. As a result both the internal structure and functioning of a successful organisation, as well as the environment in which it operates, will be in a continual state of flux. Some changes may be relatively minor and almost imperceptible, while others – such as the arrival of the Single Market – may have a much greater impact upon an organisation's activities. After having looked at the wider business environment, we try to show that organisations have to make plans to adapt to their changing business environment, and take responsibility for all of their actions.

Chapter 13 – External Influences on the Organisation examines the wide range of influences. It looks at economic, social, political, legal, technological and environmental change. The assumption is that those who make decisions should be fully aware of external influences if they are to respond positively with appropriate measures designed to meet their objectives.

Chapter 14 – The Environment of Change begins by exploring the ways of identifying and preparing for changes we might want to make as individuals. Making a change requires first the identification of needs, and then action to make sure that these needs are met. In just the same way organisations need to make appropriate plans. To do so successfully will involve utilising the knowledge, expertise and talents of their employees.

Chapter 15 – Organisational Responsibilities analyses the responsibilities which organisations have towards people who work for them, their members and shareholders, as well as other groups and individuals. This chapter explores fundamental responsibilities and, in particular, looks at the ways in which such responsibilities influence an organisation's operations.

Chapter 13 External Influences on the Organisation

Notes for OHPs

OHP 13.1 *The organisation in its environment*
This OHP refers to a term from the past! The diagram extracted from page 253 can be used when introducing the external influences upon the organisation. It attempts to show the complex intermeshed relationships of the six external influences highlighted upon the activities of the organisation.

OHP 13.2 *Objectives of government policy*
This OHP refers to the five variables of government economic policy shown in the diagram on page 260. As these are very much the traditional objectives, you may wish to follow up these five by referring to two other areas – such as balanced economic growth and social welfare.

OHP 13.3 *The circular flow*
This OHP distinguishes between the simple circular flow of income by using the illustration shown on page 261, and the more complex circular flow diagram on page 262 showing the amended circular flow.

OHP 13.4 *The Phillips Curve*
This diagram refers to pages 263 and 264 of the text. It shows the Phillips curve and describes the trade-off between unemployment and inflation.

OHP 13.5 *Fiscal policy*
In this OHP fiscal policy is briefly explained and then referred to its use in influencing demand. The illustration from page 265 showing each type of budget is then used, and underneath this each type of budget is defined.

Responses to selected Tasks and Case Studies

TASK – page 254

The responses to this task may vary widely and students should be encouraged to participate actively and develop a wide range of ideas. Make sure that the task is limited to a set period, such as the 30 minutes mentioned. At the end of this period get each group to report back. Identify the link between the effects of an external influence and having to develop a plan of action.

TASK – page 255

Try to use the answers in a practical way to relate to the simple systems model of a national economy.

TASK – page 257

Responses to this may be used as a focus for discussion throughout this section. Students should be encouraged to read newspapers, research widely and relate this area, probably more than any other, to current events.

TASK – page 258

Though Mr and Mrs Average do not exist, in order to create a valid index which can be used for statistical purposes, statisticians have to identify weightings based on the likely expenditures of an average household. A government can then identify how policies are affecting the lives of the electorate, and adjust policies accordingly.

TASK – pages 258/259

a The following figures refer to Redland:

	Original index	New index	Expenditure weighting	New index x weighting
Wine	100	50	7	350
Bread	100	200	2	400
Cheese	100	400	1	400
			10	1150

New RPI = $\frac{1150}{10}$ = 115.

b The new index shows that 'on average' prices have risen by 15 per cent.

c Weightings will need to be altered in 1989 as expenditure patterns change over time, different items have different levels of importance for different types of families, changes in prices do not affect all people equally, etc.

External Influences on the Organisation

The following figures refer to Blueland:

Eggs	100	200	2	400
Cheese	100	150	4	600
Bread	100	100	2	200
Salt	100	90	2	180
			10	1380

New RPI = $\frac{1380}{10}$ = 138.

TASK – Page 264

This particular task may be developed further and used as the basis for a work experience assignment.

CASE STUDY – New plans (page 265)

1. Some of the responses to this task are straightforward, such as the incentives under the new manufacturing investment programme which all aim to reduce taxation and are clearly supply-side. Others, such as raising the top rate of income tax, are clearly demand-side. Some are a little vague, may be argued as neither, and could be used as a basis for discussion – for example, the rules regarding takeovers.
2. Ideas will vary, according to political preferences.
3. Responses could be widely discussed.
4. Answers will vary.

TASK – page 267

Though the task asks students to find out from their local bank manager, an alternative course of action would be to ask them to obtain the appropriate banking literature from their local branch or to research this more broadly by using the banking section of the college library.

TASK – page 269

The pyramids show an ageing population with more people living longer. It will affect:
a hospitals – different types of treatment, larger numbers of patients, etc.
b schools – apart from the fall in projected numbers in the 1990s they will be largely unaffected
c banks – will need to provide more services for mature customers (e.g. pensions schemes, investment accounts)
d manufacturing companies – should be aware of the changing nature of the population – market research should identify new trends.

Task – page 269

1. Increasing unemployment seems likely to alleviate the problems of recruitment which would otherwise have been faced by employers.
2. Strategies will vary, but will undoubtedly centre upon areas such as benefits, career structure, working environment, training, opportunities.

TASK – page 272

Local authorities are generally willing to provide sets of leaflets and other literature for classroom use.

CASE STUDY – The European Court of Justice (page 274)

1. This judgement was important because it overturned recent UK legislation and it showed that the EC could invalidate laws traditionally associated with sovereignty.

2. The likely knock-on effects are resentment by the UK fishing industry, adverse public opinion against the EC and the influence the judgement has on future UK legislation.
3. The implication for organisations within the UK is that legislation designed to protect their interests is not always able to do so. Their forms of action are limited, but it may mean that they should contact MEPs or form some type of pressure group.
4. The implications for other organisations are that future legislation could be influenced if discriminatory and that we might see other EC legal influences in our society.

CASE STUDY – Technology at Seiko (pages 275/276)

1. Seiko has been influenced by the desire for accuracy, fashions for clothes, jewellery and furniture, technology, sporting trends, etc.
2. Seiko used technology to improve accuracy and to permit the use of mass production techniques.
3. For the staff of Seiko, the implications of such changes are probably improved job security, greater specialisation, division of labour.
4. Answers will vary widely. Many will undoubtedly centre upon the people aspect of technological change.
5. We have only referred to broad areas. Organisations rarely remain static. Almost anything may be interpreted as change and students should be encouraged to realise this.

CASE STUDY – Poison in the water (page 277)

Answers will vary widely for most of these questions. it may be useful to support this case with a number of annual reports in which organisations identify how they engage in activities that are sympathetic to their external environment.

CASE STUDY – Decision-making in the European Community (pages 277/278)

1. The Council of Ministers clearly has the most power because it drafts the new laws, whereas the Commission monitors the need for changes in laws and the European Parliament just discusses and then amends such changes.
2. Answers will vary widely and may provide the basis for further research and discussion of the European issue.
3. Advantages might include: less spending on national governments; greater consistency with other countries; improved competition across national boundaries; stronger body capable of greater influence on world opinion.
    Disadvantages might include: loss of sovereignty; loss of control of own legislative process; stronger countries more able to influence legislation of weaker countries.
    Advantages and disadvantages would on the whole be the same for all EC members.

THE ORGANISATION IN ITS ENVIRONMENT

OBJECTIVES OF GOVERNMENT POLICY

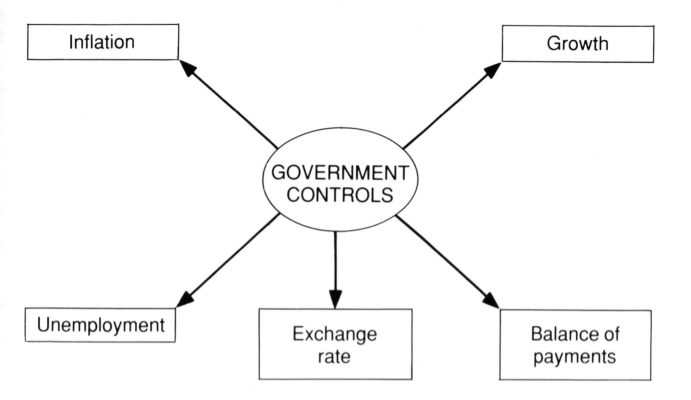

- *These five variables are the central focus for government economic policy.*

THE CIRCULAR FLOW

The simple circular flow

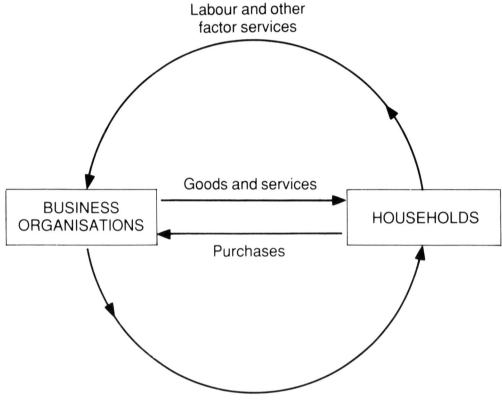

The amended circular flow

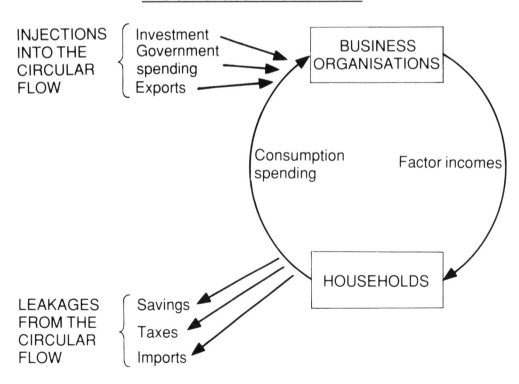

THE PHILLIPS CURVE

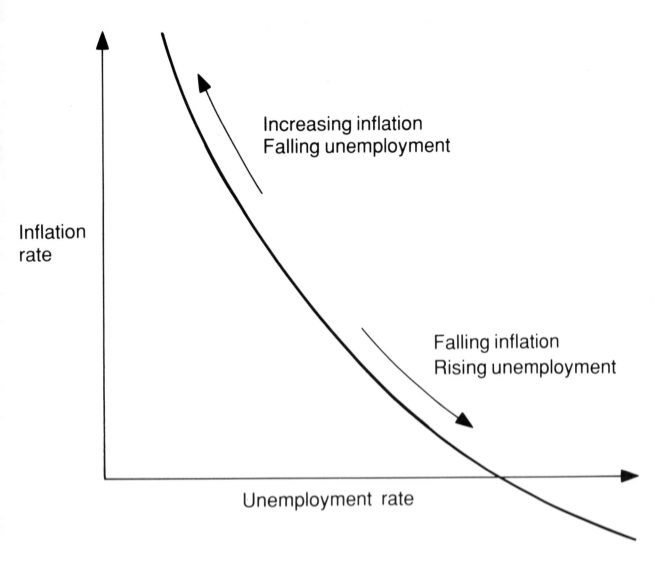

The Phillips curve is an attempt to show the relationship between unemployment and inflation. When inflation is rising unemployment is falling, and when unemployment is rising inflation is falling. The Phillips curve is used to describe this trade-off.

FISCAL POLICY

Fiscal policy is the government's policy with regard to public spending, taxes and borrowing. The government can try to influence the level of demand in the economy through directly altering the amount of spending in relation to its total tax revenues

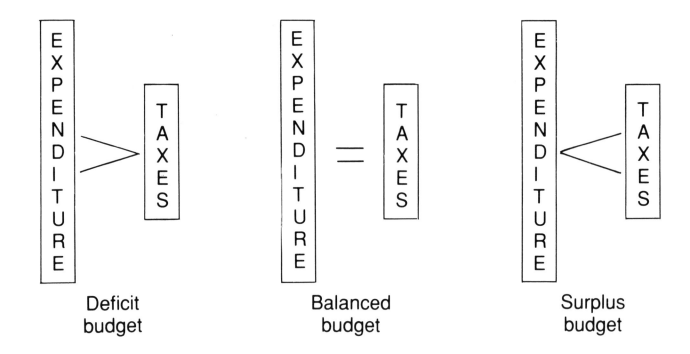

Deficit budget · Balanced budget · Surplus budget

A <u>deficit budget</u> arises when the government spends more than it takes in taxes.

A <u>balanced budget</u> describes a situation whereby the government matches its spending with taxes.

A <u>surplus budget</u> arises when the government takes in more revenue than it spends.

Chapter 14 The Environment of Change

Notes for OHPs

OHP 14.1 *Force field analysis*

This OHP accompanies the text on page 280. A short title for a problem can be written by the tutor as an overlay. For example, students may want to improve the way they work together as a team. They can work individually and then in pairs to identify all the forces that are encouraging improved group cohesion, and all the forces that are restraining group cohesion. The length of the arrows should be used to indicate the strength of the force. Once students have had time to think about the driving and restraining forces, the tutor can start to enter them on to the overlay sheet. You can ask questions such as 'Should that be represented by a short or long arrow?' Once students have agreed on a force field picture you can start to investigate ways of giving more drive to the driving forces, and weakening the restraining forces. The activity will help to encourage better team working. You can use the force field approach to a wide number of issues and problems.

OHP 14.2 *A change environment*

This OHP has been designed to accompany the text on pages 283 and 284, which looks at a wide range of changing environmental factors that affect a service station. Our OHP is used to encourage students to transfer their learning to a new business context – a corner shop. There are a lot of empty arrows that need 'filling in', so work round your group to come up with suggestions. What are the main changes in the environment of a corner shop which are likely to influence its fortunes and activities? Talk through each of your students' suggestions and fill in a completed overlay sheet.

OHP 14.3 *Forecasted employment changes in the UK*

This OHP blows up the table on page 286. It shows some major changes in the employment structure in recent years and in the future. Students are asked to identify major structural changes. Use OHP 14.6 to give some major pointers to changes. Then return to OHP 14.3 and talk through the major changes in individual industries. Wherever possible this should be related to the local situation.

OHP 14.4 *Relative importance of factors of production at different stages of the product life cycle.*

Before using this OHP, quickly review each of the factors of production identified. Also review the notion of product life-cycle. The OHP accompanies the text on pages 287 and 288. It shows the relative importance of each of the factors at different times. You should relate the diagram to specific products (e.g. different types of television sets, confectionery, well-known newspapers, models of cars). Clearly not all products will fit the simplified model outlined, but there is a considerable amount of validity in it.

OHP 14.5 *What economic union entails*

This illustration blows up the figure on page 292. You could uncover a line at a time to bring home the nature of each of the descriptions. You should relate your descriptions to the European Community. You could use this OHP as a useful way of introducing trading relations in the EC.

OHP 14.6 *Case Study – New jobs for old*

This OHP gives a skeleton of answers which can be used with the Case Study on page 286. We have already described how this should be combined with OHP 14.3.

Responses to selected Tasks and Case Studies

CASE STUDY – Changes in the textiles industry (page 288)

1 In the early 1990s the textile industry was hit by world recession. Falling incomes and rising unemployment caused households to cut back on expenditures. There was a fall in demand for household fabrics in particular (e.g. curtains, furniture coverings). As a result there was a slump in the home market. On the foreign market, British exports became increasingly uncompetitive because of the weak dollar – many exports are priced in dollars – so that earnings abroad fell. During the 1980s there had been a lot of investment in the textile industry so that in the early 1990s productivity was higher than ever before. However, there is a lot of spare capacity. Today textile manufacturers have to be highly flexible in their approach.

2 These include: flexibility; market consciousness; ability to change; ability to switch quickly to new products; a work ethic; an ability to take setbacks and adapt to meet new circumstances; a lot of enterprise; an ability to think quicker than competitors; an awareness of world trends and world markets; the ability to work with state-of-the-art technology.

3 Restraining forces include: exports are priced in dollars; Far Eastern suppliers can beat us on price and often flexibility; we do not know when the recession will end; firms that have borrowed money may get into debt; new trainees may be reluctant to enter a declining industry.

4 There should be an emphasis on flexibility and shortening lead times; changing to meet new fashion; building a research and design advantage; concentration on best lines; concentration on the strength of being close to the home market; benefiting from investment of the 1980s; continuing to invest in better techniques.

TASK – page 289

Examples of items in each category are:

Food and live animals	sheep, wool, beef, cereals
Beverages and tobacco	whisky, cigarettes
Crude materials	bricks, wood, iron ore
Mineral fuels	oil, coal
Animal and veg. oils etc.	butter, margarine
Chemicals	chlorine, acids
Manufactured goods	cars, watches, computers
Machinery and transport etc.	lorries, digging equipment
Miscellaneous manufactures	manufactures not in main groupings
Other items	any other tangible items

Section 2 – The Wider Business Environment

Chemicals, beverages, and tobacco and other items are in surplus. Others are in deficit.

Britain is a net importer of most manufactured items because other countries have a comparative advantage in their production today.

There is an overall visible trading deficit of £27530 million. This is not necessarily a problem because it needs to be placed in the context of the whole trading picture, including invisibles and returns on capital investments. For example, in many years we have had more money coming in from net invisible earnings than we have lost on visible exports. We also earn considerable profits, interest and dividends from overseas investments.

However, some people see the erosion of our manufacturing base as a long-term problem: a long-term erosion in comparative costs curtailing our ability to invest at home and abroad.

CASE STUDY – Automatic identification: bar-codes (page 295)

1 Advantages of an electronic till include: automatic stock control; reduction in costs; increased efficiency and speed of operation; automatic checks on money in till; balancing; cheap and efficient financial control.
2 Advantages to the customer include: faster service; better service; goods always in stock; lower prices; itemised till receipts.
3 Changes include: simplifies work tasks; faster work; less variety in work; fewer calculations; makes work more routine and monotonous.
4 EPOS – Prices can be changed in the database but they need to correspond to prices displayed for items.
5 The shopkeeper can: check on turnover of individual lines; may decide to increase stock of certain lines, reduce others (profit calculations needed). However, the shopkeeper must bear in mind that it may be specialist items that encourage shoppers to come and buy other major lines in bulk.
6 For directors and shareholders, bar-coding provides a competitive edge and therefore opportunities for enhanced profits. For managers, it provides a management control tool. For manual operators, it takes a lot of responsibility out of the work and perhaps a lot of the work satisfaction.
7 Manufacturers, wholesalers and retailers need to go with the leading edge if they want to survive. Clearly it is a heavy investment industry, but it is also one that reduces costs and improves efficiency dramatically.

FORCE FIELD ANALYSIS

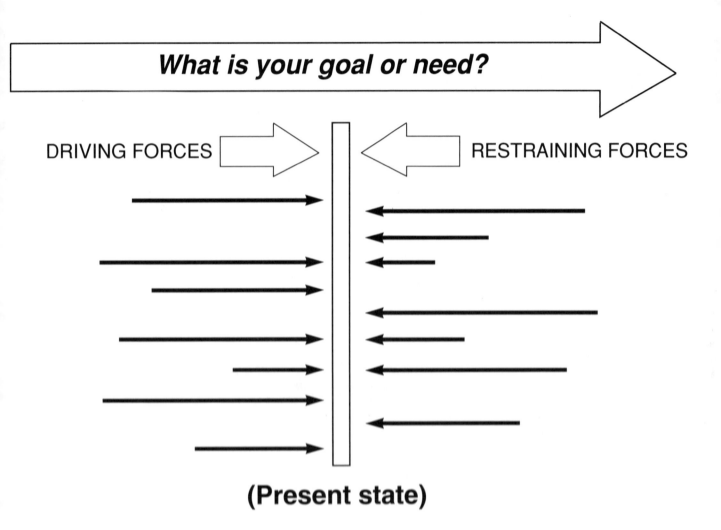

A CHANGE ENVIRONMENT

FORECASTED EMPLOYMENT CHANGES IN THE UK

	Employment in 1987	Net change 1987–95
	(thousands)	
Agriculture	558	−38
Mining	207	−34
Utilities	291	−22
Metals, minerals	443	−23
Chemicals	345	−17
Engineering	2239	−91
of which:		
Mechanical	737	−25
Electrical	567	−32
Motor vehicles	245	0
Food, drink, tobacco	581	−61
Textiles and clothing	563	−39
Other manufacturing	1102	+5
Construction	1569	+201
Distribution	5268	+414
of which:		
Distribution	3972	+97
Hotel and catering	1295	+317
Transport, communication	1500	+18
Business services	2631	+602
Other services	2420	+615
Manufacturing	5362	−230
All industries	19 807	+1523
Health and education	3001	+265
Public administration	2178	−66

RELATIVE IMPORTANCE OF FACTORS OF PRODUCTION AT DIFFERENT STAGES OF PRODUCT LIFE-CYCLE

Life-cycle phase			Factors of production
NEW	GROWTH	MATURITY	
2	3	1	Management
3	2	1	Scientific and engineering know how
1	2	3	Semi-skilled and unskilled labour
3	2	1	External economies
1	2=	2=	Capital

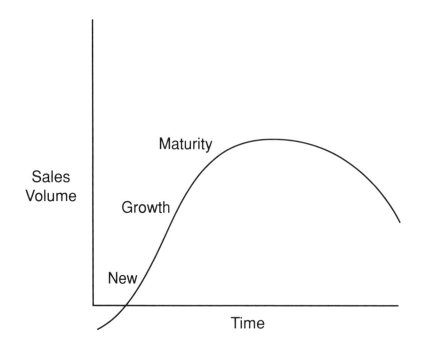

WHAT ECONOMIC UNION ENTAILS

	Removal of trade restrictions between members	Common external trade policy towards non-members	Free movement of factors of production between member states	Harmonisation of economic policies under supra-national control
Free trade area	✓			
Customs union	✓	✓		
Common market	✓	✓	✓	
Economic union	✓	✓	✓	✓

OHP 14.6

CASE STUDY: NEW JOBS FOR OLD

1   Net increase (i.e. all industries) + 1,523,000

2

GAINS	LOSSES
CONSTRUCTION SERVICE INDUSTRIES	PRIMARY INDUSTRIES MANUFACTURING

3   <u>Example: Mining</u>
   – Losses due to:
   – Exhausted seams
   – Low productivity in older pits
   – Cheap imports
   – Government preference for other fuels

   <u>Example: Business and other services</u>
   – Gains in insurance, banking, office administration etc.
   – As we become a 'third wave' economy, financial services supported by automation add value which can be exported.

Chapter 15 Organisational Responsibilities

Notes for OHPs

OHP 15.1 *Organisational responsibilities*
This OHP concentrates on the two diagrams shown on pages 299 and 300 which set the theme of the chapter. The OHP can be used to highlight a number of the internal and external responsibilities of any organisation. The illustration is in two sections; students can be invited to suggest ways in which an organisation has responsibilities to each of the groups involved and what these responsibilities would entail, and they can also be encouraged to highlight other groups that an organisation might be responsible to.

OHP 15.2 *Hazards at work*
This OHP looks at hazards at work in two of the three contexts illustrated on page 303; namely the office and the workshop. The lecturer can show the two scenes in turn, asking students to highlight the hazards shown, and asking what can be done to remove these hazards, and the responsibilities of employers and employees in the work situation (for health and safety).

OHP 15.3 *The Health and Safety at Work Act*
We feel that this OHP is particularly important. All employees and prospective employees need to develop a serious attitude and detailed awareness of health and safety regulations. The HASAW stresses the responsibility of employees as well as employers to ensure safety and the welfare of all employees. This responsibility needs to be stressed in no uncertain terms.

OHP 15.4 *How do disputes arise?*
This OHP reproduces the diagram on page 308 of the text. It shows that consumer complaints arise for many different reasons. Students and tutors can talk around this diagram. The tutor can introduce each complaint and then ask students to suggest examples as they relate to their own personal experience. The lecturer can use this OHP as a lead in to more detailed work on legal processes and how they protect consumer rights and limit the actions of organisations.

OHP 15.5 *Four competition Acts*
This OHP is designed to show that there are four main Acts that are all segments of a general policy to provide competitive markets. You will need to rotate the overhead slowly so that one segment is 'in focus' at a time. For example, start with the Fair Trading Act in an upright position. Talk it through. When you have given a general outline of this Act move round to the next segment. This should serve as a stimulating introduction to the topic. You can then tackle each of the Acts in more detail – or ask students to research them by using Tasks and Case Studies shown in the book (pages 314–320). Students should also study current cases that are hitting the headlines.

OHP 15.6 *Case Study – Exploration and production by Shell UK*
This OHP gives a skeleton of outline answers for the Case Study on pages 301 and 302 of the text.
1. *Employees* – would include the ten fatalities in 1990.
2. *Unions* – although the extract only refers to unofficial action, clearly it implies the need for effective industrial relations.
   Shareholders are implicated in the report – they would be interested in all operations written about in the report. Shareholder interest might be equally divided between sales, health and safety, environmental implications, and other factors. The need to be aware of *government interest* and pressure is suggested by the Cullen Report which called for improved safety on all offshore operations. The Report indicates that a large segment of the labour force is bought in from private *contractors* who will clearly put pressure on Shell UK to ensure safe working conditions. *Suppliers* provide maintenance and other services and components. *Customers* affect the level of sales and hence activity (note, for example, the fall in sales).
   Environmental considerations clearly create a short-term pressure to be considerate and a long-term pressure to conserve the future of the industry as well as that of the planet.
3. Here we have indicated some possible suggestions.
   For example, if pressure is put on Shell UK to improve safety standards (e.g. by unions, government, contractors), this will push up production costs, and hence reduce sales and profits.
   Customers can put pressure on Shell UK by deciding whether to buy or not because of price or other factors.
   Pressure groups can put pressure on the company from both within and without (e.g. to improve its green image).
   Every organisation has a need to maintain the goodwill of internal and external groups. Public perceptions of an organisation are likely to influence company policy.
   Today image is very important. many companies carry out image surveys to find out how the company is perceived by its publics. Clearly the results of these surveys will be fed back into policy-making at all levels.

Responses to selected Tasks and Case Studies

TASK – page 306

All of the advertisements shown would be regarded in law to be fair. They set out various job requirements (e.g. presentable and articulate, responsible, sporting background). However, they do not give any undue bias against any section of the population. The only possible grounds for complaint would be that the picture of the Fitness Instructor appears to be male.

Section 2 – The Wider Business Environment

TASK – page 308

This can be carried out as a group activity. Students could split up a page into three columns, headed 'Complaint', 'Your rights' and 'Outcome of complaint'.

By working collaboratively on the activity, students can build up a picture of their rights in a number of cases.

CASE STUDY – Ice-creams found to contain bacteria (pages 312 and 313)

This study looks at a recent food scare. Appropriate answers would be:
1. Consumers Association
2. Carries out research into a number of products; publishes results in a magazine called *Which?*; the magazine is available on subscription; it supports consumers in making complaints and offers advice.
3. a It sent inspectors round to buy ice-creams from a number of outlets.
   b It publishes results in the magazine, and the results are then publicised in the media.
4. a They buy fewer ice-creams, at least for a while. They switch from soft ice-creams to more hygienic forms.
   b They buy fewer supplies of at least some ice-creams; suffer falling sales; put pressure on manufacturers.
   c Sales decline; improve hygiene; carry out product development; advertise to improve image; some go out of business.
5. Government establishes minimum standards and legislates on production and handling of food (e.g. Food Safety Act). Can order an enquiry. Mention Health and Safety Inspectors.

CASE STUDY – A merger in the public interest? (page 318)

This study looks at a merger situation in which a number of conditions would lead to a referral to the Monopolies Commission. The answers to the questions could be:
1. The companies supplied 58 per cent of the market (well above the 25 per cent limit). The assets test states that all mergers involving combined assets of over £30 million should be investigated; in this case the combined assets are £50 million. It is a horizontal merger. The companies want to regulate resale prices. The companies want to carry out other restrictive practices (e.g. the way products are displayed).
2. It is a high-quality product and the merger sets out to preserve quality. This will benefit consumers. Product performance and quality are expected to improve.
   The UK is a world leader. Restrictive practices may benefit the UK economy both in the short and long term. Jobs will be created. UK prices are competitive when put in the context of the world situation.
   By dealing only with selected outlets, it stops the product getting into the wrong hands.
3. Much depends on what the product is. The arguments outlined above may be acceptable for some pharmaceuticals but not for chewing gum. Clearly there are many restrictive features of the agreement. The case needs to be judged on its merits. Do the benefits outweigh the costs? Suggest a few products to students – see what conclusions they come to.

TASK – pages 324/325

Benefits of fast food outlets: students need in each case to highlight who the benefits accrue to and how individuals and groups benefit. For example:
Employees – receive wages and employment
Consumers – get food, somewhere to rest their legs, a meeting place, etc.
Owners – receive sales revenue, profits, prestige, employment
Citizens – get an amenity, something to stare at, pleasant bustle, one less empty shopfront, etc.
Suppliers – custom
Local government – local taxes.

Again students need to look at the disadvantages and who these accrue to. For example:
Restaurants and other food sellers – loss of custom
Town conservationists – who may complain about the 'colour pollution' and look of a garish fast food outlet
Cleaners – who have to clean up mess and waste
Neighbours – who have to live with the noise and smell.

At the end of the day it is difficult to do a detailed analysis to see whether the benefits outweigh the costs. Wherever possible monetary values should be given to costs and benefits.

Supporting Notes for Part E – The Wider Business Environment

Further areas to explore

In looking at the wider business environment, though we mention most areas broadly, it is possible to pursue one or more specific aspects of these areas in more detail. For example, we outline the environment as an external influence, explain how it acts as an agent for change and then we relate it to an organisation's responsibilities. Although it is covered in each chapter, and supported with case analysis, it may be possible to examine one problem – such as water pollution – in more detail. Doing so may improve students' overall understanding and perception of how organisations respond to a problem, and how such a response might apply to the environmental issue.

An important aspect of the wider business environment is its topicality. This is a good area in which to introduce current issues and then examine them in great detail.

Assignment ideas and suggestions

Core Module 8 'Innovation and Change', Outcome 8.1 evidence indicator, suggests that this may be assessed by undertaking a 'case study of major change in a large organisation, identifying the factors causing change, assessing how successfully they were addressed and reporting on effects on the local area'. As an idea this is clearly very useful and important. The problem is that the success of such an undertaking really depends on the quality of information available to compile the study. The best way of approaching this is to start by gathering information from a variety of large organisations which have local operations. Write to five or six, explaining that you require information for assignment work, and then assess the response. Where you feel that you have got positive feedback, arrange to see someone and obtain as much more information as you can. See if they are prepared to come to talk to groups of students to support the assignment.

Another way to develop an assignment is to relate it to students' personal experience. For example, what external factors influence their actions? How do they manage change and what sort of approaches and attitudes do they adopt towards change? This may be a useful area to explore in the early stages of developing this theme.

The wider environment affects us all constantly. The important point is to make students more aware of many of the forces which influence their actions.

EXAMPLES OF INTERNAL RESPONSIBILITIES

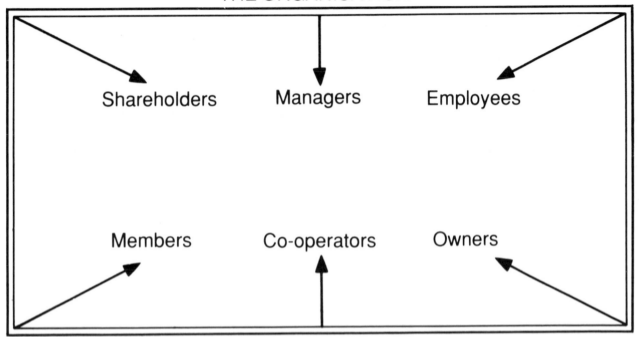

EXAMPLES OF EXTERNAL RESPONSIBILITIES

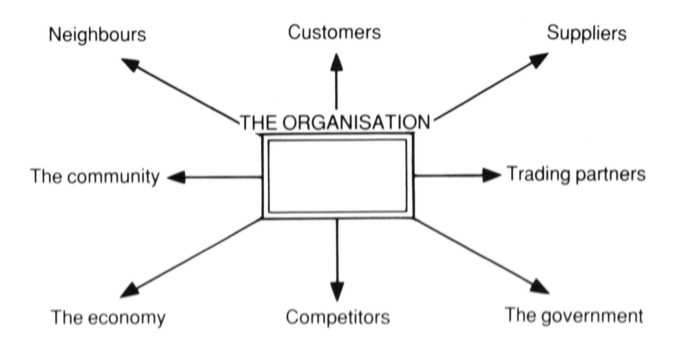

OHP 15.2

HAZARDS AT WORK

THE HEALTH AND SAFETY AT WORK ACT

This Act establishes a responsibility for both employers and employees to provide <u>safe</u> conditions at work. The employer's duty is to ensure, as far as is reasonable, 'health, safety and welfare of all employees'.

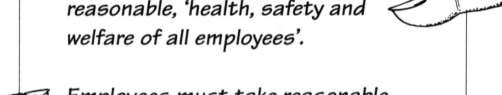

Employees must take reasonable care to ensure your own safety and the safety of others who may be affected by what you <u>do</u> or <u>don't do</u>!

HOW DO DISPUTES ARISE?

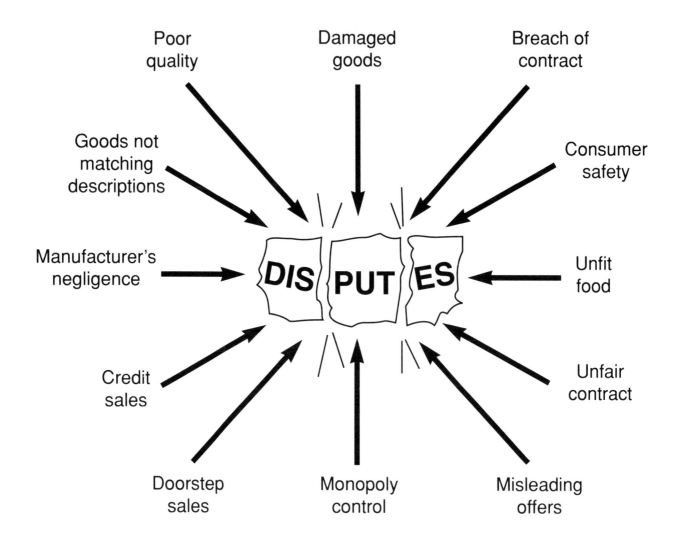

FOUR COMPETITION ACTS

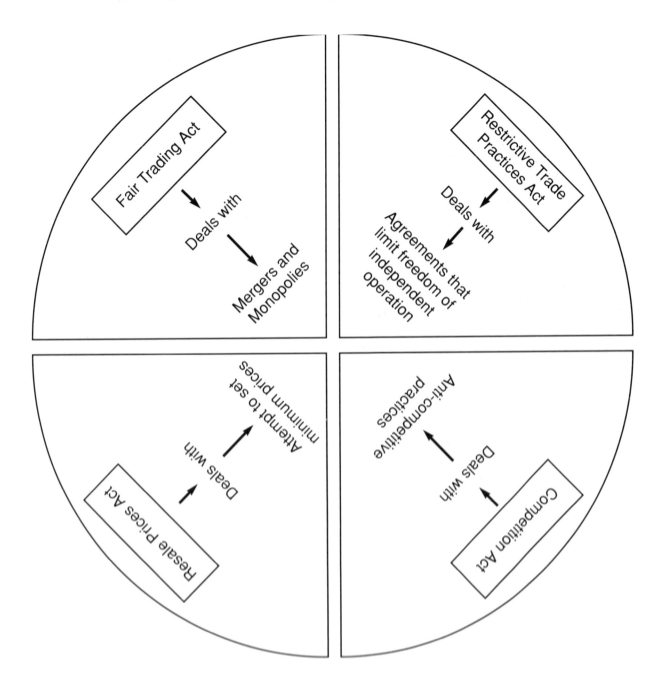

OHP 15.6

SHELL UK

1.   INTERNAL   EXTERNAL
    Employees   Government
    Unions   Contractors
    Shareholders   Suppliers
                              Customers
                              Environment

2. Employees and unions – human resource
   Shareholders – funds
   Government – legal framework
   Contractors – partners
   Suppliers – components
   Customers – purchases
   Environment – long-term future

3.
- Costs
- Custom
- Pressure
- Goodwill
- Image

SECTION 2

Part F – Managing the Organisation

This section attempts to develop a broad understanding of the requirements necessary to provide ultimate users or consumers with the goods and/or services they might require. We have entitled the theme 'Managing the Organisation' because, in order to physically provide consumers with what they want, resources have to be controlled and managed. In doing so our aim has been to create a background which might apply to either a manufacturing or service industry in either the private or public sector.

Chapter 16 – Producing Goods and/or Services is essentially concerned with the management of those operations which result in the product being available to satisfy consumer needs which have been identified by the marketing process. Engaging in such activities is the core business of all organisations and it is often argued that this function is the most difficult to understand, coordinate and carry out. Our analysis is based on the identification of five broad areas. These are product, plant, programmes, processes and people.

Chapter 17 – Making the Most of People takes the people issue further. It looks at the personnel function at work and the roles of trade unions and employer's associations. It begins by describing the path taken by an employee from the moment when he or she joins an organisation. The path consists of a number of steps, and the personnel department is concerned with the need to manage each step. The chapter also looks at other personnel functions. We examine the part played by trade unions in supporting the rights of employees, and finally look at the roles of government and the European Community in influencing working conditions.

Chapter 18 – Reviewing Performance is concerned with how organisations deal with change and concentrates upon the planning process. The text emphasises the need to monitor and review performance. It starts with hints on how to plan and review personal performance and goes on to consider organisational performance. In our changing world, all business functional areas such as marketing, human resources, production and operations, information and finance are important. In many situations they will be integrated so that an organisation can develop a better overall picture of where its competitive advantages lie. From such information it can spot opportunities and then develop a strategy to act quickly to exploit them.

Chapter 16 Producing Goods and/or Services

Notes for OHPs

OHP 16.1 *What is production?*
This OHP can be used to introduce the area of production. It defines both production and wealth creation – see page 327 – and then refers to two illustrations which further support and develop each definition.

OHP 16.2 *Types of production*
This OHP defines each type of production, and then refers to the Task on page 328 which asks students to make a short list of occupations falling under each heading. This may be used to introduce the task and then to go through various responses with students.

OHP 16.3 *Stages of product development*
In this OHP the various stages of product development are introduced, which appear on age 333 of the book. The chart depicting the elimination of choices is used and each of the steps is identified.

OHP 16.4 *Technical Operations Ltd*
This is designed to support the location task which appears on page 336 of the text. It can be used to introduce the task, show students how it works and then to go through the answers.
1. The site with the lowest costs for each 10000 components is site B.
2. The cost of removal of existing stocks in a real situation would also depend upon type and availability of different modes of transport, but it would also depend on whether the industry is bulk-increasing or decreasing, the degree of market orientation, other site benefits, the likelihood of changes in infrastructure, etc.
3. In this response students could refer to any of the other factors influencing the location of an organisation.
4. At highest cost location (C), costs will be £99750, and at the lowest cost location (B) costs will be £83362.50, representing a difference of £16387.50.

OHP 16.5 *Types of production process*
This OHP defines each type of production process and supports each with a short illustration (see pages 344–346).

Responses to Selected Tasks and Case Studies

CASE STUDY – Glaxo Pharmaceuticals (page 329)

1. A number of indicators refer to the complexity of operations at the Barnard Castle factory. For example: it employs 1500 people; tries to maintain quality; may be called upon to meet an order at short notice; 2500 preparations; 3500 purchased materials in stock.
2. These may be identified by groups and then used as a basis for discussion. The organisation approaches some of the problems of managing its operations with: emphasis upon quality; division into departments; meticulous planning; a database management system; a philosophy of 'get it right first time'.

CASE STUDY – Have the Cubans become market led? (page 330)

1. The purpose of this study is really to identify the link between market research and product research. Clearly there is a massive demand for burgers in Cuba which has prompted a relatively intransigent regime to respond with its own brand of fast food.
2. Their efforts have led to 80000 burgers being consumed daily. However, though their efforts have been in direct

Section 2 – Managing the Organisation

response to the market, surliness and incompetence could hardly be called market-led!
3 Answers will vary widely. Many Cubans might be delighted with a McDonalds, but few could probably afford to eat there regularly.

CASE STUDY – Design at Ford (pages 332/333)

1 Clearly research is widespread. It includes research into competitors' vehicles, market research into tastes, research into possible changes in legislation, etc. Each of these areas will influence the design process.
2 Areas of importance might include: engine testing; aerodynamics; safety; durability; cost; ergonomics.
3 Technology today is clearly very important. This short case refers to: CAD; computer-controlled measuring bridges; satellite communication networks; computer-linked test cell; mobile labs.

CASE STUDY – The products of the future (pages 334/335)

1 Though each of the ideas sounds futuristic, they are clearly based upon satisfying consumer needs with appropriate products. It might be worth discussing each of the ideas to identify whether these are products which consumers really require.
2 Shorter product life-cycles indicate more competitive activity and more products.
3 Answers might vary but, if the case study is correct, then despite increasing environmental concerns, we are still becoming more of a 'throw away' society.
4 Answers and ideas may vary and could be used to form the basis of a discussion.

TASK – page 338

a College – market, land, government influences, communications.
b Brewery – location of water supplies, market, services, regional characteristics, communications, transport costs.
c Bank branch – market, land.
d Car manufacturing plant – communications, government influences, land, services, transport costs, labour.
e Large supermarket – market, land, communications, labour.
f Steel plant – raw materials, transport costs, labour, safety requirements, communications, government influences.

CASE STUDY – Teesside Development Corporation (pages 338/339)

1 Teesside Development Corporation was set up because of massive structural unemployment and dereliction.
2 The Corporation aims to stimulate the economy of Teesside and to improve the living and working environments of those who live there. Students will probably refer to the nine initiatives listed on page 338.
3 a Companies benefit through the availability of sites, financial benefits, consultancy support, help with training, improved infrastructure, etc.
  b The people of Teesside benefit through the generation of jobs, environmental projects, wider interest in the area, better housing, improved infrastructure, etc.
  c The infrastructure benefits because, to bring companies to Teesside, more attention is focused on the need to develop the A1, place more emphasis upon the importance of Teesside as a port, develop air links, etc.
  d The environment benefits as, even though this means firms coming to Teesside, it means moves take place to overcome dereliction.

CASE STUDY – ZX Hardware Ltd (pages 340/341)

1 This simple exercise uses figures to emphasise the benefits of economies of scale. Though output has gone up by 370 per cent, the numbers of employees and machines have not even doubled and costs have decreased by nearly a third. These point to technical economies, managerial economies, commercial economies, financial economies etc. As a larger number of products are now being produced this points to risk-bearing economies. Such economies help ZX Hardware by providing lower costs and a larger margin, which may provide them with the flexibility to be more competitive, make larger profits and meet objectives more easily.
2 As well as output per machine and labour productivity, the figures may enable the student to identify:
  • each yearly increase in output – this may help with forecasting
  • annual increase in number of employees – figures may influence policies of recruitment, selection and training
  • machine productivity – for example, in 1989 each machine on average produced 112.5 units, in 1992 each produced 250.
3 External economies may begin to take place.

CASE STUDY – Using expert systems in purchasing (page 348)

1 An expert system is a computer program which has captured the knowledge of experts and presented it in such a way that it can be interrogated by non-experts.
2 In a purchasing department this means that problems can be analysed, processes can be explained and choices made.
3 Drawbacks could include: the loss of own expertise; employees feeling that their own views are now no longer valued; the organisation relying too heavily upon such a system.

CASE STUDY – The evolution of mass production (page 352)

1 Students may wish to discuss this. The study is intended to highlight the features of mass production and the philosophy behind it. This first task should emphasise the point.
2 Students could be advised to identify an example to help to explain their answers.
3 It meant a movement away from skilled workers towards unskilled workers.
4 It may be possible to obtain further information from: Public Affairs Department, Ford Motor Company, Brentwood, Essex CM13 3BX.

CASE STUDY – British Standard 5750 (pages 352/353)

1 The reasons for BS 5750 might include: lack of quality from suppliers; non-specified systems and procedures; insufficient market-orientation.
2 BS 5750 might influence:
  a operations – setting up systems which are more responsive to customer requirements, reduction in waste, etc.
  b the training of staff – more emphasis upon quality, communication of quality procedures, providing a wider understanding and development of the need for and use of BS 5750
  c customers – better final product, more confidence in the organisation, better value, an organisation which is more responsive to their needs.

WHAT IS PRODUCTION?

Every organisation produces goods or services (or sometimes both) as a core activity. Production is the process of making final products available for people or organisations to use. During this process wealth creation takes place.

Wealth creation adds value at every stage of production to transform inputs into finished goods, services or outputs.

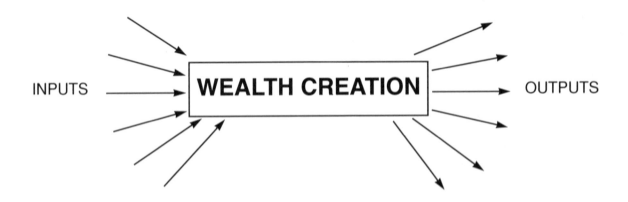

Through wealth creating activities all organisations meet their objectives

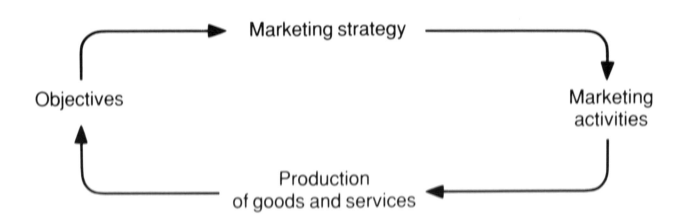

TYPES OF PRODUCTION

Primary production extracts gifts of nature.

Secondary production changes raw materials into finished or part-finished goods through manufacture.

Tertiary production provides all of the support services that make primary and secondary production possible.

TASK – Set out a table like the one below and construct a short list of occupations which fall under each heading

Primary production	Secondary production	Tertiary production	
		Commercial services	Direct services

STAGES OF PRODUCT DEVELOPMENT

A number of steps can be clearly identified in the development of a new product.

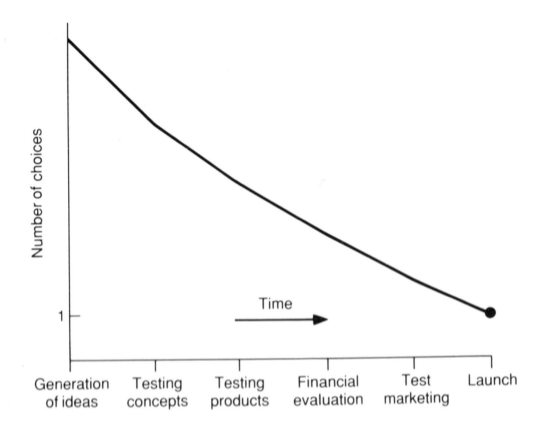

Testing concepts – involves assessing whether or not product designs might succeed in the market-place.

Testing products – involves developing models or prototypes and testing them.

Financial evaluation – assesses a new product's potential to succeed and meet objectives.

Test marketing – involves setting up a market situation as near to the real thing as possible.

The launch – is where the product is finally exposed to the market.

OHP 16.4

TECHNICAL OPERATIONS LTD

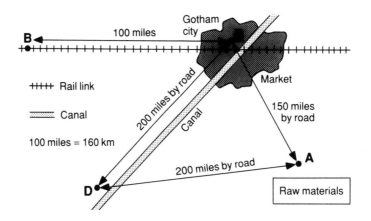

	A (£)	B (£)	C (£)	D (£)
Labour				
Raw materials transport				
Finished goods transport				
Totals				
Less government grants				
Total cost per 10 000 units				

	A (£)	B (£)	C (£)	D (£)
Labour	7300	7500	8400	7900
Raw materials transport	–	3000	2100	2800
Finished goods transport	2700	1200	–	2000
Totals	10000	11700	10500	12700
Less government grants	–	2925	–	3175
Total cost per 10 000 units	10000	8775	10500	9525

TYPES OF PRODUCTION PROCESS

Job production is the manufacture of single items by one operative or teams of operatives.

Batch production refers to a specific group of items that go through a production process together. As one batch finishes another batch starts.

Flow production is a continuous process of part-finished products passing on from one stage to another until completion.

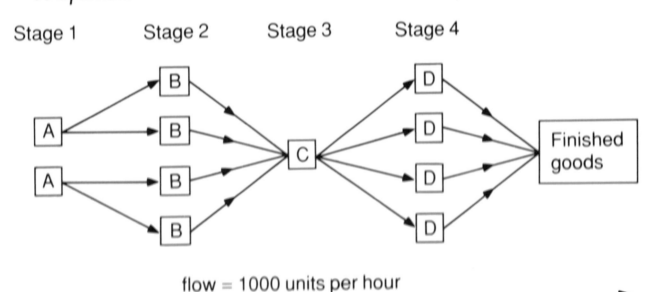

Section 2 – Managing the Organisation

Chapter 17 Making the Most of People

Notes for OHPs

OHP 17.1 *The role of personnel*
This OHP is designed to give the tutor the opportunity to give a broad overview of personnel functions. The starting point is the employment procession. The OHP has been constructed so that you can work down the page, giving brief descriptions of each of the responsibilities of personnel in dealing with employees, from recruitment to termination. You can then give an overview of other areas covered by personnel – major examples of which are given in the box in the corner.

OHP 17.2 *Tasks to be performed by shop assistant*
This OHP supports the Task on page 355. Students will have carried out the Task either individually or in groups. You will then ask them to make presentations of their suggestions. You can use the OHP which is split into three clipboard sections to answer the three questions set in the text. Clearly students will come up with a range of valid alternatives to those given in this specimen answer.

OHP 17.3 *Features of a job advertisement.*
This OHP repeats the advertisement for a Director of the New Globe Theatre Company on page 357 of the text. You can use it to highlight each of the features of an advert mentioned in the text. You can then contrast this with some others that you or the students have clipped from newspapers. Perhaps you will set a new task for students to design (or redesign) a job advertisement.

OHP 17.4 *Recruitment and selection of older employees*
This OHP suggests answers to the B & Q Case Study on page 359 of the text. We emphasise the qualities that B & Q is looking for.

OHP 17.5 *Interview checklist*
This accompanies the text on page 360. You will want to use this OHP when talking to students about interview techniques. Work down it one column at a time. Discuss each of the Dos and Don'ts, drawing on your own experiences and those of the students.

OHP 17.6 *Challenges*
This OHP looks at a range of challenges facing trade unions. Each point can be discussed and elaborated on. Work round the diagram in a clockwise fashion, giving details (see pages 370–371 of the text). Draw on recent information from the press as well as your own and students' experiences.

Responses to selected Tasks and Case Studies

CASE STUDY – A job at Mothercare (page 356)

This study draws on the earlier notes in the chapter relating to job analysis and job description.
1 Job analysis has revealed that there is scope within the organisation for an Area Manager in Southern England. There are 20 stores in the South of England that need to be regionally managed. The Area Manager will be the line manager to a number of Store Managers and will need to be aware of local trends and features of the South. The post requires leadership qualities, as well as the ability to manage change. The analysis of the post reveals a need for someone with problem-solving and entrepreneurial qualities. Clearly the post requires someone with the ability to take on responsibility and to develop new ways of tackling problems and dealing with people.
2 The job description sets out:
- title of post
- prime objectives of position – to be responsible for 20 stores in South of England, to lead a team of Store Managers, to manage change, and to maximise sales
- managerial responsibilities – Area Manager of 20 stores; to lead and motivate team
- range of decision making – coordination of selling operation; coordination of store management
- source of supervision – accountable to National Manager
- Responsibility for assets – for stores in southern England.
3 The advert is clearly set out. Perhaps it lacks pictorial stimulus and could say more about Mothercare. Students can be asked to discuss what sorts of people might respond to the advertisement and what these people might be looking for. Are these ingredients contained in the advertisement?
4 A few examples might be: prospects of post holder; where the post would be located; what counts as appropriate retail experience.

TASK – page 365

This task asks students to identify a number of well-known unions.

Manual	ASLEF	Associated Society of Locomotive Engineers and Firemen
	NUM	National Union of Mineworkers
	TGWU	Transport and General Workers Union
	NUPE	National Union of Public Employees
	EETPU	Electrical, Electronic, Telecommunications and Plumbing Union
White collar	NUT	National Union of Teachers
	APEX	Association of Professional Executive, Clerical and Computer staff
	NALGO	National Association of Local Government Officers
	NASUWT	National Association of Schoolmasters and Union of Women Teachers
Managerial and Professional	NATFHE	National Association of Teachers in Further and Higher Education
	BALPA	British Air Line Pilots' Association

CASE STUDY – Out of tune (pages 367/368)

This study looks at a dispute between the ROH and the Musicians' Union. The answers to the questions depend on the sort of bargaining stance that the management want to take – confrontation or conciliation.
1 There are a variety of possible answers. If the prime concern is to guarantee that performances continue it will be necessary to keep discussions open (i.e. not to appear to be 'locking out' musicians). The management could agree to some independent arbitrator or conciliator (e.g. through ACAS). Perhaps management and employees need to sit down to discuss contractual agreements. Management needs to make employees clear as to what the major difficulties are in granting an increase of more than 5.5 per cent. Clearly there is a range of alternative possibilities if management is to be more confrontational.

2   Union members have already worked to rule (lengthening intervals) and carried out a token strike (missing a rehearsal – although this may be a lockout). They could win public support through lobbying the media and the public. They could take more intense strike action. They could extend their go-slow to arrangements such as taking more time getting to their seats. They could refuse to work overtime. They could carry out a sit-in, etc.
3   This is an open question. Clearly there are advantages in going to arbitration in that you are opening up the case for an independent decision. However, you may find the financial implications difficult to swallow if it goes against you. In a way it would be better to reach an 'in-house' arrangement as clearly the two parties need to work closely in the long term. The article mentions that the union wanted to avoid strike action.

CASE STUDY – Changes in the labour force (pages 368/369)

This study encourages students to explore some of the implications of changes in the working population for trade unions. The materials show there will be an increasingly ageing working population (particularly an increase in the middle-age range).There will be a small increase in the number of men and a large increase in the number of women available for work. The number of men available for work under the age of 34 will fall by about three-quarters of a million.

1   The changes described above are likely to accentuate other changes that are taking place in the UK's industrial structure. Heavy industry and manufacturing continue to decline, as do the numbers of people in trade unions. Male full-time workers in heavy industry have in the past been the group which is most highly unionised. The size of manual trade unions is likely to contract (e.g. unions in mining, engineering, steel, fishing). At the same time we are likely to see more members in unions such as banking, local government, teaching, shop working. A number of unions will be likely to merge so that we have more general unions made up of people from several trades – as numbers fall off unions may seek to retain a power base in this way. White collar unions, and unions seeking to attract part-time employees, are likely to expand. Generally, as the number of people in unions falls, so too will their influence. The service unions will become more influential than unions representing manufacturing industry.
2   Unions will need to look at the benefits they are offering members. They may need to concern themselves with relevant issues (e.g. fighting for the provision of pre-school nurseries, flexitime and crèches). They will need to show that they are interested in creating better opportunities for part-timers; to take on board 'womens' issues'; to look at the provision of leisure opportunities; to consider 'image' and 'mission'; to rethink aims and strategy; to look at ways of attracting and retaining membership; to look at who their members are and identify their needs. Unions will then be able to target their recruitment more effectively.

CASE STUDY – A single-union deal (pages 371/372)

This study highlights recent trends in UK industrial relations towards compromise between unions and managers to secure stable working conditions. It is an example of a number of single-union deals that have recently been struck.

1   The employers have contributed: secure (stable) employment (i.e. job guarantees); employee representatives on the board; higher than average wages.
2   The AEU had contributed: total flexibility between skills; a commitment to high productivity levels; the opportunity to deal with just one union; clear procedures to resolve disagreements (an independent appeal body, followed by a ballot of members).
3   The employers will benefit by stable production conditions, high output levels, relatively long hours worked, low unit costs of production, good labour relations.
    The employees will benefit by high wages, stable working conditions, secure terms, brighter prospects, etc.
    Local businesses will benefit from having an affluent body of consumers to buy local products.
    Suppliers of components will benefit from supplying components for 200000 cars a year. Car purchasers will benefit from being able to buy cheap, well-made cars.
    The British economy will benefit from producing cars that are exported, with a large proportion of the factor costs (e.g. wages) being earned in this country.
4   Potential weaknesses of the deal are: it excludes other unions; employees may be exploited in the longer term; profits and dividends will go to Japan; it involves working for longer that the desired 37-hour week.
5   The deal can be seen as forward-looking in that: it is based on co-operation rather than conflict; it involves employee participation in decision making; it looks to future prosperity and investment; it creates flexibility and multi-skilling; it is the sort of deal that encourages a long-term competitive edge.

THE ROLE OF PERSONNEL

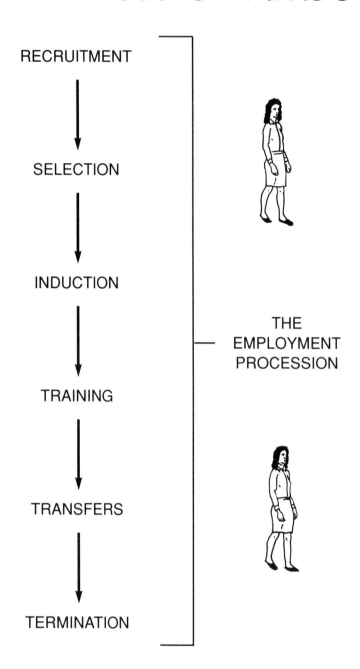

RECRUITMENT
↓
SELECTION
↓
INDUCTION
↓
TRAINING
↓
TRANSFERS
↓
TERMINATION

— THE EMPLOYMENT PROCESSION

PERSONNEL ALSO RESPONSIBLE FOR

HEALTH AND SAFETY
EQUAL OPPORTUNITIES
BARGAINING
APPRAISAL
DISCIPLINE
PAYMENT

TASKS TO BE PERFORMED BY SHOP ASSISTANT

What tasks?
- Shelf stocking
- Till duties
- Answering queries
- Stock pricing
- Shelf tidying

Skills and Qualities
- Clear communication
- Pleasant manner
- Read fluently and make calculations
- Bend and lift
- Get on with people

Skills acquisition
- Training "on" and "off" the job
- Layout and stacking of goods
- EPOS training
- Customer relations
- Teamwork

FEATURES OF A JOB ADVERTISEMENT

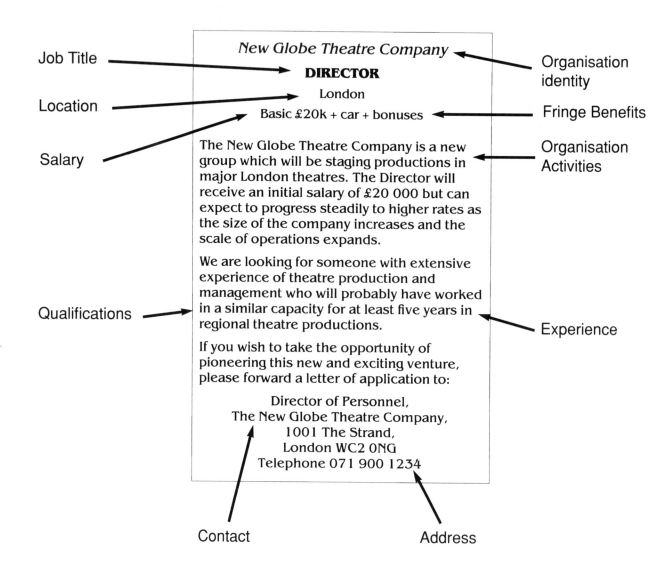

RECRUITMENT AND SELECTION OF OLDER EMPLOYEES

1 Reliability, maturity, willingness to work, prepared to stay with the job, knowledge and experience of DIY materials

2

QUALIFICATIONS and EXPERIENCE	Ability to communicate and knowledge of DIY materials
ATTITUDES	Reliability, and willing to work Pleasant manner
PHYSICAL	Good health, basic manual skills

3 B & Q's experience is that – for jobs at this level – older staff tend to be more reliable, knowledgeable, and dependable.

4 As average age increases, B & Q may suddenly lose a lot of staff. Some tasks (e.g. lifting) may require younger employees.

INTERVIEW CHECKLIST

DO	DON'T
Find out about the firm before the interview	Be late
Dress smartly but comfortably	Smoke unless invited to
Speak clearly and with confidence	Chew gum or eat sweets
Look at the interviewer when speaking	Answer all questions 'yes', 'no', or 'I don't know'
Be positive about yourself	Be afraid to ask for clarification if anything is unclear
Be ready to ask questions	Say things which are obviously untrue or insincere

CHALLENGES

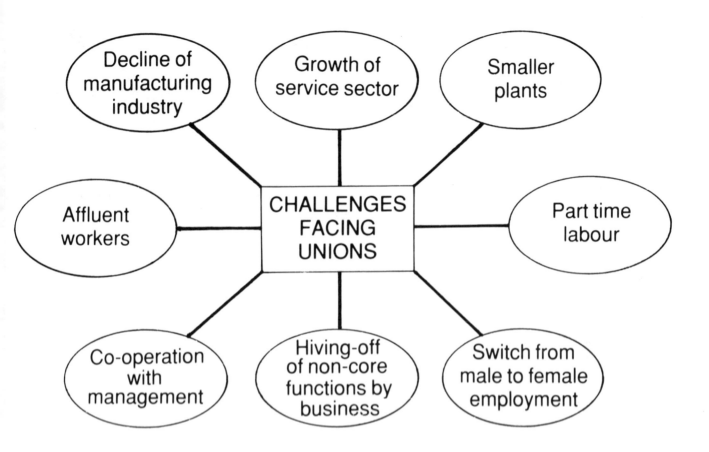

Section 2 – Managing the Organisation

Chapter 18 Reviewing Performance

Notes for OHPs

The final chapter sets out to bring a number of threads together. The OHPs therefore focus on a range of planning instruments which will be helpful to all learners.

OHP 18.1 *Devising a personal action plan*
All students will need to develop personal action plans. This OHP will be of great value in briefing groups of students. It covers only the major headings, so tutors will need to work down the OHP, drawing out the main points which are made on page 378 of the text.

OHP 18.2 *Controlling by means of feedback and corrective action*
This OHP looks at how control mechanisms can serve the effective functioning of a particular system. You can initially take the student along the pathway from input, through processes to output. This can be related to any production system (e.g. the manufacture of a new type of biscuit – see notes on systems in Chapter 1).
You can then move to the top of the diagram to show how important it is to establish initial performance standards. These standards might relate to the size, texture, quality of the biscuits, etc. These standards need to be fed into the system so that comparisons could be made between the actual product and the required product.
You can then review the diagram again starting from inputs, to processes, showing that measurements of performance will need to be made (e.g. quality control standards – checking by an electronic eye, manual testing, etc.). If the performance at any stage of production fails to meet the standard set, then corrective action will need to be taken (perhaps less sugar needs to go into the mix) – processes need to be adjusted.
Finally you can review the whole diagram, relating it to other production systems. Perhaps students can suggest alternative systems that would fit the model outlined.

OHP 18.3 *The whole organisation plan*
This OHP shows the nature of whole organisation planning. This involves integrating all systems planning within the organisation The OHP can be used to link together the various sub-systems. Organisational planning helps to bring objectives out into the open. Each sub-system should be directed towards the same goal so that plans are interwoven. You should first uncover the diagram at the top and ask students what each of the systems would embrace and what would be the main priorities of each of the sub-system plans. As students work across the diagram you can uncover new segments of the text down the page.

OHP 18.4 *A planning approach*
This OHP looks at a useful approach that can be used to develop organisational planning. The OHP needs to be tackled a section at a time in order to explain each of the areas involved (see pages 383 – 384 of the text). The OHP can then be re-worked, looking at a particular planning issue. For example, it could be used to tackle an issue related to the course: How can students improve the quality of the assignments they produce? or How can work experience placements be used more effectively to fit in with coursework requirements?

OHP 18.5 *Managing change*
This relates to pages 385 and 386 of the text. It tackles the important area of managing a change – particularly one involving a number of members of an organisation. This OHP can be used most effectively when it is related to a familiar change process. Students can be asked to introduce a particular change and relate it to the procedures given in the text.
Students may find the following suggestions (from Rosabeth Moss Kanter, a colleague) on building commitment to change helpful:
- Allow room for participation in the planning of the change.
- Leave choices within the overall decision to change.
- Provide a clear picture of the change, a 'vision', with details about the new state.
- Share information about change plans to the fullest extent possible.
- Divide a big change into more manageable and familiar steps; let people take a small step first.
- Minimise surprises; give people advance warning about new requirements.
- Allow for digestion of change requests – a chance to become accustomed to the idea of change before making a commitment.
- Repeatedly demonstrate your own commitment to the change.
- Make standards and requirements clear – tell exactly what is expected of people in the change.
- Offer positive reinforcement for competence; let people know they can do it.
- Look for and reward pioneers, innovators and early successes to serve as models.
- Help people find or feel compensated for the extra time and energy change requires.
- Avoid creating obvious 'losers' from the change. (But if there are some, be honest with them early on.)
- Allow expressions of nostalgia and grief for the past – then create excitement about the future.

OHP 18.6 *Your work experience*
This summarises the Case Study on page 379 of the text. Talk through it with students to debrief some of the learning outcomes of work experience which have helped students to think more clearly about career choice and development.

Responses to selected Tasks and Case Studies

TASK – page 377

It is helpful to specify a particular type of shop worker, teacher, nurse, hairdresser (e.g. a sales assistant, midwife, trainee hairdresser). Some competencies are straightforward. for example, for a shop assistant: can operate a till; can make simple numeric calculations; can answer queries accurately; can direct complaints to correct channel; can stack shelves in orderly fashion.

However, it is important to point out to students that it is important to establish competence objectives in a clear fashion so that the person carrying out the task is absolutely clear about what is involved.

A competence objective is a combination of three elements:
- The task – what the trainee or person carrying out the task will do.
- The conditions – how the task will be carried out.
- The criteria – what standards will be achieved before a trainee or person carrying out the task will be judged competent at the task.

The task element describes what someone will actually do. An example of a task element might be that a trainee will be able to 'word-process a business letter'. This describes what the trainee will do.

The next stage is to give more information about how that task will be completed. These are the conditions under which the task will be carried out. The main conditions are likely to refer to any equipment that will be used, and a stimulus or starting point such as a problem which needs to be resolved, or a customer request. Using the work-processing example, conditions are that: (a) the equipment is a word processor, and (b) the starting point is an uncorrected manuscript, or rough draft.

Our objective is now to: *word-process a business letter given a word-processor and an uncorrected manuscript or rough draft.*

Finally you will need to specify the standards to be achieved. How will you and the person carrying out the task know and agree that s/he has successfully completed the task?

The criteria should include any factors that are crucial to the successful completion of the task. The main criteria will include: the standards which are required of the end product; any time limit which is given; the degree of accuracy required; whether the task must be done in any give sequence; whether any particular procedures must be observed (e.g. safety). In our example the criteria might be: (a) correct all errors, and (b) display the word-processed information centrally.

So the final competence objective is: *word-process a business letter given a word-processor and an uncorrected manuscript or rough draft, correcting all errors and displaying typewritten information centrally.*

Working with the sort of guidance outlined above, students can begin to develop competence objectives in a more rigorous fashion.

TASK – Difficulties in drawing up competency statements (page 377)

This task follows on from previous ones. Students will readily appreciate that not all tasks can be described in simple competencies. In teaching, for example, it may be easy to establish competencies for effective use of the overhead projector and the development of presentation skills. However, it is not so easy to present material in a way that will interest different types of audience or to be able to communicate clearly to a range of ability levels. The teacher who has learnt all the practical skills of teaching may find her/himself faced by an alienated audience, in a classroom which is poorly resourced, teaching a group of students studying at the wrong level.

It may be difficult to develop competency statements for researchers into novel areas, or for those doing tasks that nobody has done before. How could you draw up competency statements for an artist? Clearly there are some simple competency statements that could apply to any occupation, but there are others that are indefinable (e.g. the trickery of Paul Gascoine, the passion of Elizabeth Taylor).

CASE STUDY – Changing corporate priorities (page 384)

1 Many of Bellamy's suggestions are sound and quite simple to understand and put into practice. For example, the notions of 'fishability' and 'swimability' are common sense measures that most people would agree to. There are already enforceable regulations covering cleanliness of water. It makes sense for all businesses to consider ways of minimising waste and recycling any waste products. Putting water intakes downstream of outfalls may not affect industrial users in that they do not always need clean water.

Many people would argue that it would make more sense for businesses to develop broad environmental strategies and to develop action plans based on these strategies – rather than the other way round (in the way Bellamy indicates). Many companies do already carry out environmental audits although these are frequently criticised for glossing over the truth.

Again, it makes sense to develop environmental management systems and to make sure that policies filter down to all staff. This should be achieved by Total Quality Management. Companies should support British Standards if they are to be effective.

2 If companies are to adopt such suggestions in their planning, initiatives will need to come from board level.

3 Yes, in many organisations there is still much to be done towards effective environmental concern. It seems likely that, with increasing consumer and governmental concern for the environment on a global level, all companies will need to incorporate environmental protection into their core purposes. This will need to become an implicit part of mission statements.

4 Strategic planners will need to consider best use of organisational resources in conjunction with best care of the environment. Profitability, and other business goals, will have to be related to sustainability of resources in the long term. Strategic thinking will need to relate goals and priorities to a broader picture of growth and success. A strategic audit looking at what has been achieved and what is likely to be achieved must consider the green perspective.

Operational planning will need to take aboard such issues as training, action planning, auditing, response to auditing, organisation of new management systems, creation of environmental affairs teams, the development of quality programmes, etc.

Control mechanisms will need to be set out to measure pollution and other spillover effects caused by an organisation, coupled with ways of responding to any irregularities and ways of correcting problems. Quality control mechanisms must be established, providing standards. Comparisons need to be made against standards to ensure that standards are kept. Every organisation will need to establish environmental standards and ways of ensuring that these standards are complied with.

5 The simple answer is all systems. Marketing will need to respond to changing needs in the market place. Finance will need to develop new methods of green accounting which account for negative effects of activities. Production will clearly be affected – from packaging, to ingredients, to waste disposal. The human resource will have to be protected from harmful activities at work, as well as being trained to minimise harm to the work environment.

6 There are several approaches to this. Students should consider who would need to be convinced and how; who are the most important decision makers, how can they best be reached?

7 Again this involves looking at the change process. Constructive persuasion is needed on a wide front – media, business community, consumers, etc.

Section 2 – Managing the Organisation

Supporting Notes for Part F – Managing the Organisation

Further areas to explore

The avenues to explore are endless and constantly subject to wide-ranging changes, innovations and developments. It is certainly worth scanning the professional press, such as *Director* magazine, *Personnel Today*, marketing magazines etc., to find out about current ways of thinking so that you can regularly update and develop your input. The more topical the area is made, the more relevant students will find the materials to their own immediate working environment.

Another way of developing this area is to bring specialist speakers into the classroom to speak to students about their particular brand of management. One way of doing this is to invite Understanding Industry to integrate their programme of speakers into your course. UI will assess your needs and then develop a programme which invites senior managers from a variety of areas into your college to talk about carefully identified areas – such as human relations, operations management and management. Visits involve eight sessions which can be organised on any basis and be made to fit into the college timetable. A great benefit of the UI course is that it can be developed to establish regular links which may be of use in a variety of different ways. UI can be contacted at Enterprise House, 59 – 65 Upper Ground, London SE1 9PQ
(Tel: 071 620 0735).

Assignment ideas and suggestions

This area is very suitable for a major group activity based on a real or simulated organisation. One difficulty, however, is coordination, particularly if you have a large number of both part-time and full-time students and if the activity involves a visit.

The activity should refer to the ways in which organisations cope with innovation and change. This will enable students to bring in, develop and pull together elements from nearly all parts of the course and gives them the flexibility to develop areas which they view as being important.

DEVISING A PERSONAL ACTION PLAN

- Area for development
- Person responsible for implementing change
- Task group
- Statement
- Roles
- Analysis of needs
- Action steps
- Evaluation

OHP 18.2

CONTROLLING BY MEANS OF FEEDBACK AND CORRECTIVE ACTION

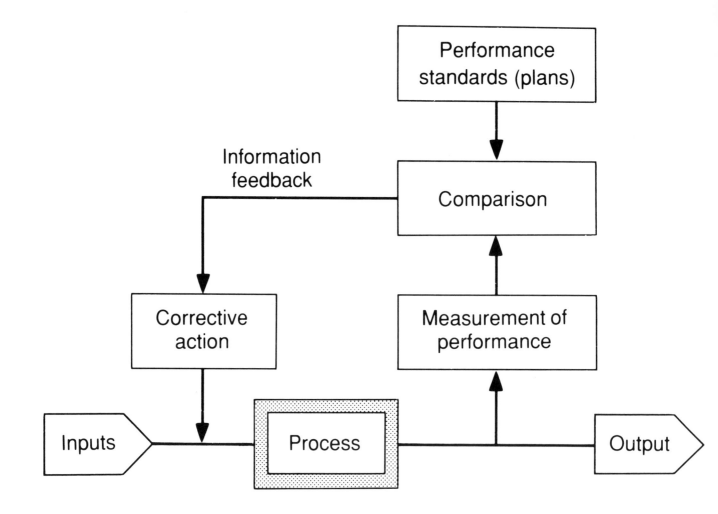

OHP 18.3

THE WHOLE ORGANISATION PLAN

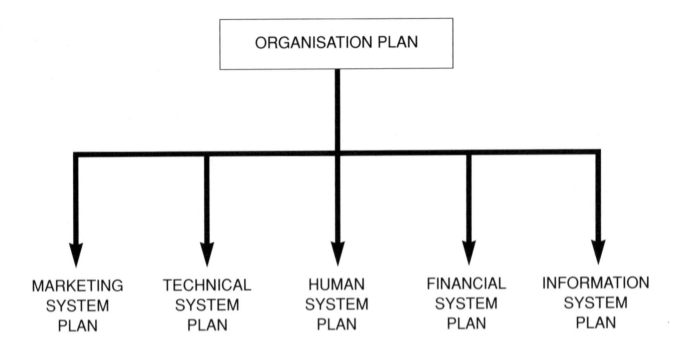

- *Marketing* aims to keep organisation aware of consumers.

- *Production* aims to use resources in best way to meet market needs.

- *Personnel* aims to keep organisation in tune with its 'people'.

- *Administration* aims to service organisation with effective procedures.

- *Finance* aims to provide long-term and short-term finance.

- *Information system* aims to process data effectively and provide communications.

OHP 18.4

A PLANNING APPROACH

? Diagnosis → Where are we?/Why? (audit)

? Prognosis → Where are we going?

? Objectives → Where do we want to go?

? Strategy → What is best way to achieve objectives?

? Tactics → What actions are needed to meet short-term targets?

? Control → How far have we come? (performance indicators)

MANAGING CHANGE

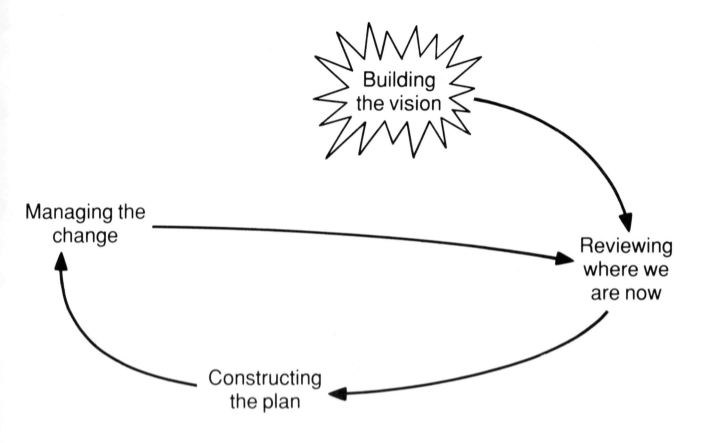

- **Building the vision** What is it? – Why should we do it?
  When and where can it be built?
  How do we manage it.

- **Reviewing** Current provision (audit)
  Resources
  Roles and responsibilities
  Development needs

- **Planning** Policy statements
  Action plans
  Commitment

- **Implementing** Carrying out plan
  Securing permanent change

YOUR WORK EXPERIENCE

☆ How has it helped you to think about career development?

1. Describe the job

2. Who were you responsible to?
   What were you responsible for?

3. How have you benefited?
   a. Knowledge of work
   b. Improved skills/aptitudes
   c. Changed attitudes
   d. New career plans
   e. Understanding of working world.

GLOSSARY

accountant
prepares business accounts, arranges finance and gives financial advice to clients and/or colleagues

accounts clerk
assists accountant in preparation of accounts, collection of cash and paying bills

accrual concept
recording a transaction in the period to which it relates and not necessarily when paid

acid test ratio
tests for ability of business to pay its debts soon: liquid assets/current liabilities

appropriation account
describes how profit is used, either distributed as dividends or retained as reserves

assets
items that continue to have value – i.e. can generate future cash receipts

audit
external check of financial accounts to report whether 'true and fair'

bad debts
goods/services were sold on credit, but customer now thought unlikely to pay. Charge as an expense in the P&L and reduce debtors correspondingly

balance sheet
summary of assets, liabilities and capital at a particular point in time

bank loan
money lent by a bank for interest

bank overdraft
amount of money taken out of current account in excess of that paid in

budget
an estimate of future revenue or expenditure. May include a P&L, balance sheet and cashflow etc.

capital
the total stock of wealth owed to the shareholders. Sum of money originally invested plus profits made and retained since trading started

capital employed
can be defined by looking at either side of the balance sheet. Either 1) share capital plus long term liabilities or 2) total assets less current liabilities

capital expenditure
money spent on fixed assets

cashflow statement
describes where money comes in from and where it is paid out to for a period

consistency concept
similar items should be treated consistently from one period to another. E.g. stock valuation and depreciation policies must not change from one period to the next

corporation tax
tax on company profits

cost of sales
direct cost of goods sold (including material, direct workers and other direct costs)

creditors
amount due to suppliers for goods/services received on credit

current assets
cash or any other asset that will be converted into cash during the next 12 months

current liabilities
overdraft and other amounts owed (including creditors) repayable within 12 months

debentures
long-term loan with fixed repayment date, e.g. in five years time. Interest is usually paid annually and must be paid before shareholders receive dividends. Debentures are often secured on a business asset like a building

debtors
sales on credit for which the customer has not yet paid. Included under current assets in the balance sheet

declining balance method
depreciation on fixed assets calculated as a percentage of the declining net book value. Using this method assets are depreciated proportionately more during the first few years of use

depreciation
process of writing off the value of a fixed asset over its economic life. Depreciation is charged as a cost in the P&L and the fixed assets valuation in the balance sheet is reduced correspondingly

dividend
amount of profits distributed to the shareholders. Profits not so distributed are 'retained' as 'reserves'

Glossary

dividend cover
net profit after tax/dividend – this ratio shows how many times over the dividend could have been paid. The higher the ratio the greater the amount of earnings retained for future investment

dividend yield
dividend per share/market price – use gross dividend to compare with other investment opportunities like bonds or bank accounts

earnings per share
net profit after tax/average number of ordinary shares

equity
another term for shareholder's capital, i.e. share capital plus reserves

expenses
costs incurred on goods or services that are no longer of value

FIFO
first in first out method of stock valuation. Charge to the P&L the stock items purchased first

finance director
head of finance department and sits on company's board of directors

financial accounts
prepared to satisfy legal reporting requirements – results in issue of 'published accounts' to company shareholders

finished goods stock
production has made materials into a company product ready for selling

fixed assets
assets purchased not for resale but for use over a long period (over 12 months). Required for company to do its business, e.g. buildings, and motor vehicles

freehold land and buildings
properties owned by the company

furniture, fixtures and fittings
miscellaneous fixed assets like desks, shelving and electrical wiring

gearing ratio
long-term liabilities/equity capital

going concern concept
assumption that company will continue trading in the foreseeable future. Very important as valuation of industry-specific equipment and stock may be very low if the company is to be wound up

gross profit
sales – cost of sales

hire purchase
method of purchasing an asset on credit, but title to goods does not pass to the buyer until all instalments have been made

historical cost
transactions and assets are recorded at original cost value

inflation accounting
adjust accounts to reflect changes in price levels

intangible assets
a valuable item that has no physical form. E.g. patents, goodwill, leases

interest
compensation to lender of money for loss of use, risk of non-repayment and inflation

invoice
document showing goods sold. Used by both seller and buyer to maintain records of business transactions

lease
contract to allow the lessee to use an asset leased from a lessor (usually the asset's owner). Results in the payment of a regular rent

leasehold land and buildings
property rented under a lease contract from the freeholder

liabilities
amounts owed to others

LIFO
last in first out method of stock valuation: cost of sales based on the price paid for the most recently purchased items of stock

liquidity
extent to which liquid assets (cash and debtors) are available to pay liabilities

long term capital
sources of finance not repayable for at least five years

management accounts
to provide accounting information to managers to help them make decisions about the running of the company

market price per share
the price at which shares in the company are currently bought and sold. (On the Stock Exchange in the case of a listed PLC)

net book value
difference between cost of a fixed asset and its accumulated depreciation (i.e. amounts charged to P&L since purchased)

net current assets
current assets – current liabilities
(i.e. working capital)

net loss
occurs when sales are less than cost of sales plus expenses

net profit after tax
gross profit less expenses less tax

net profit to sales ratio
net profit/sales

net realisable value
sales value of an asset less costs of actually selling the asset

nominal share value
par value of share unrelated to its market value. E.g. nominal value of a Marks & Spencer share is 25p

operating profit
also called 'net profit' (before interest) and 'trading profit'

ordinary share capital
total value contributed by ordinary shareholders who participate in the ultimate risks and returns of business

plant and machinery
equipment usually used in the direct production of the business's goods. E.g. a lathe or moulding press

preference shares
entitled to a fixed rate of dividend with right to be paid before ordinary shareholders. They have limited voting rights

prepayments
amounts paid in advance to the period for which benefit will arise. E.g. paying rates for year ahead and telephone rental for three months ahead

price earnings ratio
market price of share/earnings per share (after tax)

profit and loss account
accounting statement calculating the net profit for the period

profit margin
net profit (before interest and tax)/sales

provision
created in anticipation of a future asset write-off or a potential liability. E.g. a customer may not have paid his debts for a long time so a 'bad debt provision' may be created

prudence concept
important principle used by accountants when the outcome in terms of a profit or loss looks uncertain. They tend to look on the pessimistic side

ratio analysis
expressing one variable in relation to another and comparing the result with ratios for other firms in the industry and with past results for the firm

raw materials
materials still in the unprocessed state received from suppliers

reserves
generally amounts of profits not paid out to shareholders as dividends

residual value
estimated value of a fixed asset at the end of its economic life

return on capital employed
net profit (before tax)/capital employed

revaluation reserve
net amount by which assets are revalued over historical cost

sales
revenue from selling goods or services

secured loan
lender has legal right to be repaid, if the company is in default, by selling the asset on which the loan is secured

share
the capital of a company is split into many shares to make ownership easily tradable

share premium account
proceeds of a share issue in excess of the nominal value of the shares sold

Glossary

shareholders' funds
share capital plus reserves

stock
goods bought for resale. Includes raw material, work in progress and finished goods

stock turnover
cost of sales (pa)/stock value

straight line method
describes where fixed assets are depreciated equally over a number of years

trading account
part of the profit and loss account: sales less cost of sales equals gross profit

trading profit
also called net profit (before interest) and operating profit

turnover
same as revenue or sales

Value Added Tax
customs and excise levy (currently at 17.5%) on sales of many items

vertical format
modern format of balance sheets with shareholders' funds vertically below net assets

work in progress (WIP)
describes materials partly manufactured into finished products. The value of work in progress includes direct labour costs, overheads such as management costs and transport costs already incurred

working capital
another term for net current assets

working capital ratio
current assets/current liabilities

write-off
to charge as an expense in the profit and loss account rather than hold in the balance sheet as an asset

Heinemann Educational
a division of Heinemann Educational Books Ltd,
Halley Court, Jordan Hill, Oxford OX2 8EJ

OXFORD LONDON EDINBURGH
MADRID ATHENS BOLOGNA PARIS
MELBOURNE SYDNEY AUCKLAND SINGAPORE TOKYO
IBADAN NAIROBI HARARE GABORONE
PORTSMOUTH NH (USA)

Copyright © Dave Needham and Rob Dransfield 1993

First published 1993

A catalogue record for this book is available from the British Library on request

97 96 95 94 93
10 9 8 7 6 5 4 3 2 1

ISBN 0 435 455249

Designed by Ken Vail Graphic Design

Printed by Athenaeum Press Ltd,
Newcastle upon Tyne

All rights reserved. The pages for use as overhead projections may be copied for use within the institution for which they have been purchased as may the student activities on pages 111–121 and the glossary on pages 173–176. Under no circumstances may copies be offered for sale.